Orchestrating Collaboration at Work

Orchestrating Collaboration at Work

Using Music, Improv, Storytelling, and Other Arts to Improve Teamwork

Arthur B. VanGundy • Linda Naiman

JOSSEY-BASS/PFEIFFER
A Wiley Imprint
www.pfeiffer.com

Copyright © 2007 by Arthur B. VanGundy, Ph.D. and Linda Naiman
Originally published by Pfeiffer, An Imprint of John Wiley & Sons, Inc., 2003.

Certain pages from this book are designed for use in a group setting and may be reproduced for educational/training purposes. These pages are designated by the appearance of the following copyright notice at the foot of the page:

Reproduced from *Orchestrating Collaboration at Work* by Arthur B. VanGundy & Linda Naiman with permission of the copyright holders. Copyright © 2007 by Arthur B. VanGundy, Ph.D. and Linda Naiman

Terms: This notice must appear on all reproductions as printed.

This free permission is limited to the paper reproduction of such materials for educational/training events. It does not allow for systematic or large-scale reproduction or distribution (more than 100 copies per page, per year), electronic reproduction, or inclusion in any publications offered for sale or used for commercial purposes—none of which may be done without prior written permission of the copyright holders, or authorization through payment of the appropriate percopy fee to the Copyright Clearance Center, Inc., 222 Rosewood Drive, Danvers, MA 01923, (978) 750-8400, fax (978) 750-4470, or on the web at http://www.copyright.com.

Requests to the Publisher for permission should be addressed to:
Arthur VanGundy, 428 Laws Drive, Norman, OK 73072. (405) 447-1946,
email: avangundy@cox.net.

To order additional copies of this book:
Please contact BookSurge, LLC or www.Amazon.com
1-866-308-6235, Email: orders@booksurge.com

Library of Congress Cataloging-in-Publication Data

VanGundy, Arthur B.
Orchestrating collaboration at work: Using music, improv, storytelling, and other arts to improve teamwork / Arthur B. VanGundy, Linda Naiman. Includes bibliographical references.

ISBN: 9781419651748

1. Teams in the workplace. 2. Arts and society. 3. Organizational change—United States. I. Title: Orchestrating collaboration at work: Using music, improv, storytelling, and other arts to improve teamwork. II. Naiman, Linda. Title.

HD66 .V355 2003
658.4'02—dc   21 2002154067

Cover art: Mike Reed/Images.com
Cover Design: Linda Naiman
Interior Design: Bruce Lundquist
Illustrations: Linda Naiman and Lotus Arts

Printed in the United States of America

Praise for Orchestrating Collaboration at Work

It goes without saying that no company, large or small, can win over in the long run without energized employees who believe in the mission of their company and understand how to achieve it collaboratively. Top innovative companies already know what CEOs and top managers realized from the four day World Economic Forum in Davos, Switzerland held in January 2006 --- innovation and creativity are critical to the future success of their companies. To compete in this fast globalizing world, people with higher cognitive and affective (emotional) thinking skills need to be hired.

We as educators can do our part. The creative and innovative process is all about the attitude, energy and enthusiasm we put into it to make it happen. We can look at *Orchestrating Collaboration at Work* as another book of training activities, or, as one of the Fisher Price Toys ads suggest, the opportunity to Play, Laugh and Grow. Thomas Huxley once said "The secret of genius is to carry the spirit of childhood with you into maturity." It takes one little spark of inspiration to breathe life into whatever we do. That is the competitive advantage.
— Mireille Massue, *Training Media Review*

...A welcome breath of air... This is well worth the $48.99. [e-book edition] I have spent many times that amount to go to week-long conferences that didn't give me anywhere near this much useful
information.
—Renee Hopkins Callahan, director of Innovation Services, Decision Analyst, USA

For inspiration incorporating improvisation, role playing, and storytelling into your retreats, we recommend *Orchestrating Collaboration at Work*. [It] contains several excellent exercises that use storytelling and improvisation that help groups explore important issues. For our money there is no better book on how to use art forms effectively in a retreat setting than *Orchestrating Collaboration at Work*.
— Merianne Litemen et al, *Retreats that Work*

Our experiences today, obviously demonstrate the need for a holistic, integrated approach to value creation. Only by means of interdisciplinary dialogue and action will we be able to access the existing multitude of creative development opportunities in social, ecological and economic contexts. *Orchestrating Collaboration at Work* provides hands on examples on how to start and facilitate such a process.
— Andreas J. Harbig, partner, head of strategic HR management,
Pricewaterhousecoopers, Germany

High-performance collaborative work teams are the new performance imperative in both private and public enterprises. VanGundy and Naiman show how using the arts to unleash the creative potential of individuals and teams will allow this new performance mandate to be met. This book helps to push the edge of the arts-in-business envelope.
— Robert F. Lusch, dean and distinguished professor, The Neeley School of Business,
Texas Christian University, Fort Worth, Texas

I think your book is wonderful!! You masterfully designed a terrific array of resource materials.
— Susan M. Osborn, PhD, faculty, organizational systems, Saybrook Graduate School and Research Center, Folsom, California

VanGundy and Naiman bring a unique blend of creativity and art to provide practical techniques for increasing and improving teamwork. With this book, I am no longer afraid to explore the exciting world of the arts in business. My only regret is that they didn't write it ten years ago.
— Sivasailam "Thiagi" Thiagarajan, director of research, QB International

A wealth of enablers in the form of training exercises:
I have discovered the power and the simplicity in finding/applying a wide variety of experiential exercises that spark creativity and imagination in groups. The beauty of this valuable workbook is that it unleashes our hidden potentialities. I have successfully used these activities in private business and in non profit organizations and in every occasion the results have been the creation of high energy and relevant discoveries among participants. Thank you Arthur and Linda for your valuable contribution.
— Carlos Mota Margain, OD consultant, Mexico

Will VanGundy ever run out of creativity?
 Arthur VanGundy has already given us just about every conceivable aid to creative work — from "Brain Boosters" to "101 Games" and "101 Activities." Now with Linda Naiman he delivers the most comprehensive and accessible creativity and innovation resource for groups I've ever seen. And it's about time someone got business people to start thinking like artists. Anyone in business creativity, ideation, and new-product development will find the VanGundy-Naiman approach not only inspiring and fun but incredibly effective. This binderful of brilliance would be a bargain at $900.
— Peter Lloyd, creativity consultant, USA

Terrific resource
I've purchased MANY books filled with MANY activities over the years. This is one of the best I've seen. It has lots of immediately applicable activities that are practically guaranteed to succeed. As well, it triggers lots of additional ideas for additional activities, too. A tremendous resource that every trainer, facilitator and consultant should add to their library.
— David Gouthro, consultant, Canada

I dedicate this book to my mother and grandmother VanGundy, who introduced me to the arts; my undergraduate professors, who refined my appreciation; Thiagi, who inspired me from afar; my co-author, Linda Naiman, for expanding my interest in the arts in business; my daughters Sarah and Laura; my granddaughter Chloe; and to Janet J., my special "dramatic" friend.

Arthur VanGundy

I dedicate this book to my father for encouraging me to be an artist; my mother for teaching me adventure; Ruy Paes-Braga, Wal van Lierop, Miha Pogacnik, and Arthur (Andy) VanGundy for taking a risk and opening doors for me; and to all those who have the courage to make life a work of art and work a work of art.

Linda Naiman

Acknowledgments

We first would like to thank all of the contributors to this book who provided their time and expertise on arts-based training. This book would not have been possible without them. We also want to thank the visionaries who generously shared their wisdom, especially John Seely Brown, Margaret Wheatley, Miha Pogacnik, Nick Nissley, Todd Siler, David Whyte, Richard Olivier, Gael McCool, Nan Crawford, Michael Dawids, Deborah Jacroux, Thiagi, Paul Smith, Jerry Kail, and Bob Root-Bernstein. Finally, we are indebted to our editors at Pfeiffer who contributed to different stages of this project: Josh Blatter, Samya Sattar, Kathleen Dolan Davies, Martin Delahoussaye, Dawn Kilgore, and Susan Rachmeler. Their advice, encouragement, and especially their patience, helped us to endure the months of writing and editing.

Contents

1   Introduction and Overview   1

        Activity Format   3
        Learning Objectives   4
        Organization of the Book   4

2   Orchestrating Collaboration Using the Arts   6

        What Do We Mean by "Arts"?   7
        Why Use the Arts in Business?   8
        How Can We Apply the Arts to Business?   9
        Learning to Collaborate   11
        Examples of the Arts as a Vehicle for Collaboration in Organizations   12
        Why Use the Arts in Corporate Training?   17
        Debriefing an Arts Experience   20
        Do Some Art Forms Work Better Than Others in Different Work Groups?   21
        Guidelines for Conducting an Arts Experience   21

3   Getting Acquainted and Icebreakers   23

Getting Acquainted
Chairs   24
More Than 1,000 Words   27
Personality Typing   29
Sing, Sing a Song   34

Icebreakers
Belly Dancing   37
Building Community   39
Check In   43
Inspiration Rituals   48

4   Arts Warm-Up Activities   51

Abstraction and Composition   52
Art Gallery   56
Arts Expedition   58
Express Yourself   64
If Your Face Were a Poem   67
Restrictions and Limitations   69

Strike Up the Band 71
Thinking Symbolically 74
Transparency 77

5   Collage/Mixed Media 79

Candid Collages 80
The Figure/Ground of Conflict 83
Golden Moment 87
Just Suppose Juxtapose 89
Mapping Your Future 92
People Wall 95
Searching for Genius in All the Unexpected Places 98
Self-Portrait 102
Shift Happens 106

6   Drawing 110

Commentated Pictures 111
Drawing You into Conversation 114
Metaphorical Thinking 116
Picture Switcher 119
Symbolic Code 122
Vision Quest 126

7   Music 129

Bamboos 130
Group Groove 133
Jazzin' It 136

8   Painting 138

Getting Graphic 139
Spheres of Influence 141
Visual Symphonies 144

9   Poetry 147

Limerick Your Learning 148
Poetry in Motion 151
Rhyme and Reason 155
Rhyme Time 158

10 Storytelling 162

Exchanging Perspectives   163
Fictionalization and Imaginative "Restoryation"   166
It's History   170
Once Upon a Team   172
Stories of Change   176
Story Lines   180
Story Weaving   183
Time Capsulle   186
To Go Where No Group Has Gone Before   189

11 Theater Improvisation 194

The Advocates   195
The Answer Is Always Yes   198
Ball Toss Chaos   200
Free Association Word Ball   204
Obstacles and Opportunities   206
Reflections   213
Statues   216
Team Moving   219
Two Minutes of Fame   223
The World's Worst Leader   229

12 Miscellaneous Activities 232

The Blue Ribbon Panel   233
Collaboration Imagination   236
Here's Looking at You   242
The Innovative Product Award   245
Mythical Animals   248
Teams in Motion   250

13 Evaluation Activities 252

Artistic Insights   253
Song Lyrics   255
Symbolic Solutions   257

Contributor Contact Information   260

About the Editors   264

1 Introduction and Overview

We live in a world that is increasingly complex, chaotic, and confusing. The challenges we face require creativity and innovation at every level of organizations. For organizations to flourish, we must create environments that foster creativity in all its diversity. We must bring together multitalented groups of people who collaborate and orchestrate the exchange of knowledge and ideas that shape the future.

We cannot find all answers to our problems in the world of the rational, logical, and scientific. We need to bring other competencies into the equation: creative, artistic, imaginative, symphonic, and mythic. These competencies largely have been ignored in contemporary organizations. There is growing awareness, however, that they are vital to organizational success.

Margaret Wheatley[1], author of *Leadership and the New Science*, contends:

> "If we don't start to learn as leaders who people are, what they are capable of, what their potential is, how creative most people can be in the right circumstances; if we don't learn all this, then we are not going to succeed. I'm hoping that leaders will come to realize, that even though they work under awful pressures these days, they can't keep driving organizations by numbers. A profound shift in our culture has to take place; and providing the kind of orchestration that evokes our creativity and brings out the best of each person's talent, is a very powerful metaphor."

---

[1] Wheatley, M. *Interview with Linda Naiman, 2003.*

The arts always have enriched human experience by reflecting back to us who we are and what we stand for and deepening our understanding of ourselves, each other, and the world in which we live. The arts lead us to wisdom and truth. This is why art is both revered and feared. As Nan Crawford, director of Pacific Playback Theatre, notes:

> "Since human organizations are fundamentally driven by human behavior, the arts are a vast resource providing understanding for human relationships, the way we communicate, our motivations, our limitations, our resolve, our capacity to envision possibilities, and our ability to manifest our goals. What an organization doesn't address regarding relationships can become their competitors' strategic advantage. Forward thinking leaders can gain tremendously practical tools by applying wisdom and skills from the arts to their current business issues. Creating collaborative environments—where people feel connected, where their voice is heard and their creativity is cultivated—is not only healing, it is a strategy for success."

Brandweek[2], a publication for marketing and branding professionals, notes:

> ". . .to understand the process of creative genius, it is valid for business people to look at the model of the artist. The business of the artist is to create, navigate opportunity, explore possibility, and master creative breakthrough. We need to restore art, the creation of opportunity, to business."

A growing number of companies in the UK, Europe, and the United States are using the arts to enhance organizational performance. Some of the companies that have used the arts as a tool for visioning, communication, customer service, and team development include: American Express, AT&T, BBC, Kodak, Boeing, British Airways, Coca-Cola, Daimler-Chrysler, Dell Computers, Ericsson, Halifax, Hewlett-Packard, Honeywell, IBM, Kodak, Lever Faberge, Lockheed Martin, Marks & Spencer, Mattel, Nike, Pfizer, Saatchi & Saatchi, Sears, Shell, Skandia, and the World Bank.

This book is designed for trainers, facilitators, consultants, educators, and managers who provide training of all types to employees. Its purpose is to provide nontraditional ways to achieve more traditional training goals involving teamwork. Specifically, this book is designed to create new participant perspectives by allowing them to access their often-hidden creative abilities. The activities are intended to achieve this goal by using various arts to provoke more creative outcomes. Strategic goals can be achieved only with sustained, focused team efforts.

---

[2] Column by Annette Moser-Wellman, February 23, 1998. BPI Communications, Inc.

when the level of group energy begins to decline. You could modify all of these to provide more team-focused experiences. However, their primary value lies in introducing participants who do not know each other and as general warm-up activities.

The activities in Chapter 4 are designed to help participants feel more confident about expressing themselves artistically and to ease them into the collaboration activities. The goal is for them to perform with more comfort and proficiency in the art form involved. No prior artistic ability is assumed. However, as with any group activity, the experiences can be enhanced if individuals first have a chance to "loosen up" their artistic minds. All creative activity requires a period of preparation, be it meditative or simply "playing" with objects or concepts. For instance, "doodling" is one form of preparing for a drawing.

The arts-based activities designed specifically to enhance team collaboration start in Chapter 5 with collages and mixed media—piecing together of often disparate concepts and materials to produce a unique creative product. It is followed by Chapters 6 through 11, which present, respectively, activities based on drawing, music, painting, poetry, storytelling, and theater improvisation. Chapter 12 presents miscellaneous activities using design, photography, and sculpture. Finally, Chapter 13 contains three post-training activities using drawing, music, and storytelling.

Activity Format

Each activity uses the same headings: "Objectives," "Uses," "Art Form(s)," "Time Required," "Materials, Handouts, and Equipment," "Procedure," "Discussion," and "Variations" (an optional category). A more detailed description of these headings follows:

- *Objectives:* Describes the primary purpose of an activity. Enhancing team collaboration, of course, is the overriding purpose of each activity, but there also may be secondary objectives.

- *Uses:* Lists other ways to apply an activity. Not all possible uses will be listed for each activity, so feel free to use your imagination.

- *Art Forms:* Represents the primary art form used for an activity, as well as related or secondary art forms. For instance, an exercise classified as involving dance also might involve music or improvisational theater.

- *Time Required:* Refers to the total amount required to complete an activity, including a group discussion. Of course, the number of groups and participants may cause variations in the times listed.

- *Materials, Handouts, and Equipment:* Whatever is required to complete an activity, such as paper, pencils, paint, flipcharts, computers, arts supplies, and handouts providing additional information.

Learning Objectives

After using this book, we hope you will:

- Understand how to use the arts to enhance training outcomes
- Learn how to unlock and tap the hidden potential of employees
- Teach others specific skills for individual, group, and organizational effectiveness
- Incorporate the content, form, and structure of the arts to resolve business problems
- Provide training activities that participants should find more stimulating than traditional ones
- Provide new insights to employees regarding how their behaviors affect others
- Inspire trainees to express themselves openly and creatively
- Create new perspective for employees to use to resolve business problems

Organization of the Book

This book is similar to other compilations of training exercises for groups; it differs, however, in the sources used to create the activities. *Orchestrating Collaboration at Work* represents somewhat of a revolution in that all seventy activities are crafted using arts-based principles. Painting, collage, poetry, improvisational theater, storytelling, and other arts serve as a foundation for the activities and for enhancing team collaboration. The arts can create the perspectives needed to integrate training concepts and improve team interactions. These activities also may help improve group creativity, communication, leadership, problem solving, and other traditional training outcomes.

To provide a context and a rationale for the arts in business, Chapter 2 contains insights, observations, and advice excerpted from interviews with such arts practitioners as business author Margaret Wheatley, poet David Whyte, actor Richard Olivier, PARC scientist John Seely Brown, researchers Nick Nissly and Bob Root-Bernstein, and artist Todd Siler. Their comments offer innovative and transformative insights for applying the exercises. This chapter also attempts to answer such questions as, "What do we mean by the arts?" "Why use the arts in business?" "Why use the arts in corporate training?" and "What are some guidelines for conducting arts experiences?"

Chapter 3 contains four arts-based getting-acquainted exercises and four icebreakers. You might use the getting-acquainted exercises for groups who have not worked together much or who may be resistant or feel uncomfortable with training exercises; use the icebreakers at the start of a session or

- *Procedure:* Describes the steps for facilitators to use to implement an activity. These are not "etched in stone." Experienced facilitators especially should feel free to modify the steps for different situations.

- *Discussion:* Questions to ask the participants to facilitate a discussion about the activity and its applicability to team collaboration. This section also might include comments about the art form and its value in enhancing team performance.

- *Variation(s):* This is an optional heading that will not be included with all activities. Be sure to read the variations when they are included, since you may find an optional procedure better suited to your needs.

At the end of each activity, we also identify who created it. We made an effort to include a variety of arts practitioners to increase the diversity and, we hope, the quality of the activities. A brief bio is included with each activity, and contact information for each contributor can be found at the back of the book.

2 Orchestrating Collaboration Using the Arts

> "If the group is an art form of the future, then convening groups is the artistry we must cultivate to fully explore the promise of this form."
> —*Centered on the Edge*, 2001, Fetzer Institute

We live in a global society that uses teams to create wealth, market share, customer service, competitive advantage, and other markers of organizational success. Teams provide the social "glue" in organizations that melds together people, processes, and technologies to produce services or products. Organizations cannot function without teams; however, teams must be designed properly to fit organizational cultures. And they must be managed properly, a topic that has consumed countless management theorists over the years.

Organizations need teams to produce creative products, just as artists need the tools of their work. There may be a science to orchestrating team collaboration, but there also is an art. Artists often cannot predict the outcomes of their creative endeavors any more than managers can predict outcomes for their team challenges. Management "science" is necessary and contributes practical theories for teams to work better together. A more balanced approach, however, might blend science with art and magnify team effectiveness.

Orchestrating the efforts of team members to collaborate together represents an art form itself. Team leaders can be viewed as "conductors" who must facilitate individuals producing an optimal "composition" for every task. However, team leaders and facilitators should not orchestrate teams the way we often view musical conductors orchestrating symphonies. According to Ben Zander, conductor of the Boston Philharmonic Orchestra, the traditional orchestra conductor metaphor of team leadership may be inappropriate. In a December 1998 interview in *Fast Company* magazine, he notes that musical conductors are mostly "dictators" with unquestioned authority. He proposes, instead, that conductors would be better served to empower their musicians to be the best they can be. So too should team managers, leaders, and facilitators.

This book is designed to bring out the collaborative power of teams through different applications of the arts. It is important, therefore, to explore first what is meant by the arts and how the arts can be applied to teams in organizations. This chapter will look at the nature of the arts, the existence of art, the rationale for using arts in business and in organizational training, provide a discussion on how some arts forms might be better than others, give guidelines for conducting an arts experience, plus bring out several other topics.

To gather information to discuss these topics, co-author and artist Linda Naiman contacted some of the leaders and pioneers in the arts-in-business movement. Many of them generously agreed to be interviewed via telephone, email, and in person. What follows is some of the richness of thought she gleaned from these interviews. She also has injected her own commentary about the arts to supplement their perspectives. The discussion begins with an examination of what constitutes the "arts" and art.

What Do We Mean by "Arts"?

The arts encompass the visual art forms of drawing, painting, sculpture, architecture, photography, electronic media, design, and video as well as the performing arts, which include dance, storytelling, poetry, music, film, and theater.

How Do We Know Whether It Is Really Art?

While aestheticians have not been able to agree on a definition of art (or beauty, for that matter), it generally is agreed that art is characterized by originality of thought, technical excellence, and a theoretical grounding. *The Encyclopedia Britannica* defines art as "the use of skill and imagination in the creation of aesthetic objects, environments, or experiences that can be shared with others" (www.britannica.com/eb/article?eu=9772, September 20, 2002).

Many would argue against these definitions, because art isn't necessarily beautiful. Art that breaks away from established conventions can be experienced as vulgar, shocking, and disturbing—yet it still is art. Igor Stravinsky's "The Rite of Spring" was so revolutionary in its use of primitive rhythms and its radical break from established conventions, it caused a riot on opening night in Paris in 1913. Gillian Wearing, a rising star in the contemporary art world, explores the world of drunken squalor of troubled young adults in her wall-sized video aptly titled, "Drunk." British art critic Mark Beasley describes her work as "the aesthetics of degradation." Beauty and ruin create a disturbing paradox. Sometimes we need to be disturbed to break out of apathy and complacency.

Leo Tolstoy, in his essay, "What is Art?" (1896), asserted:

> "Art is not, as the metaphysicians say, the manifestation of some mysterious idea of beauty or God; it is not, as the aesthetical physiologists say, a game in which man lets off his excess of stored-up energy; it is not the expression of man's emotions by external signs; it is not the production of pleasing objects; and, above all, it is not pleasure; but it is a means of union among men, joining them together in the same feelings, and indispensable for the life and progress toward well-being of individuals and of humanity. In order correctly to define art, it is necessary, first of all, to cease to consider it as a means to pleasure and to consider it as one of the conditions of human life."

Why Use the Arts in Business?

Richard Olivier, former director of the Globe Theatre (UK) and author of *Inspirational Leadership, Henry V and the Muse of Fire,* notes:

> "Logical planning and implementation have got business where it is—it will not take it where it needs to go in this millennium. The call for flexibility, imagination and creativity at work is growing every year. And these are the mainstays of the creative artist. As we say to the business folk we work with: 'Actors and artists have lived with insecurity for hundreds of years. Now it's your turn!'"

According to Bonnie Goren, training manager of a large U.S. news organization:

> "Some of the greatest difficulties business leaders face revolve around the need to instill passion, gather energies toward a common vision, and motivate change in employees. Traditional communication methods between leaders and staff typically do not reach deeply into employees—where passion, vision, and ability to change reside. The arts have the potential to touch the minds and hearts of employees, and truly engage them."

Deborah Jacroux, a work/life consultant with the Microsoft Corporation (USA), says:

> "Over the years the logical/analytical left brain has dominated business decision making. Skills that utilize intuition, inspiration, and active imagination haven't found a home within the corporate world. Many employees have equally separated their love of creativity and the arts, and a chasm exists between their right and left brains. The arts convey stories and the opportunity to enter a place where all is possible. The major obstacles corporations currently face, such as

diversity, cross-group collaboration, and work/life balance, all can be met with an increased focus on the arts.

What is art, if not the enactment of diversity? All art, whether the visual arts, spoken stories, or the grace of dance, expresses the rich variety of authenticity of culture—a tapestry of humanity already painted for our eyes to read as symbol and understand with our hearts. Work rises from the soul and sculpts our future using creative imagination. Corporations of the future that understand the creative impulse within the human spirit will be the leaders of tomorrow."

How Can We Apply the Arts to Business?

The worlds of the arts and business are formulating a new relationship, distinct from the traditional models of entertainment or sponsorship. As Miha Pogacnik, a concert violinist and cultural ambassador to Slovenia, argues: "The world of arts must be rescued out of the prison of entertainment and the world of business must be led out of the desert of dullness of meaning!" In this new relationship, art is a role model for business, since all great art pushes boundaries beyond the established norms. Thus, it can teach us about aesthetics, ambiguity, diversity, chaos, change, courage, and complexity. According to British aesthetician, Sir Herbert Read, "The artist's task is to break through the limitations of previously codified knowledge, to lead humanity to the future."

Businesses today want to break away from their limitations, aim higher, and be a creative force for the greater good of the world. We need the transformative experiences the arts give us to thrive in a world of change. In ancient cultures, the mystery schools put students through initiations to overcome fear, learn something about their true nature, and gain self-actualization (self-mastery). The arts give us a taste of the mystery and help make sense of the world.

Trainer Marlene Caroselli notes:

"We study the arts and artists whose reason-for-being is to look at what everyone else is looking at and see what no one else sees. [Paraphrased from Gorki.] Artists, for example, serve as a bridge. (Leaders do as well.) They bridge the current with the past, the past with the future, the old with the new, the tested with the unexplored. Artists rebel. They refuse to conform. They seek a better way. Such attitudes lie at the heart of the quality movement, predicated on a faith in continuous improvement."

Many of the people interviewed for this book asserted the need for deeper levels of conversation or for different kinds of conversation. Margaret Wheatley said:

"I don't think we notice how much we've lost by this dead language that we use and the jargon that we use, until we have an artistic experience and realize that life is so much richer, lively, funnier, sadder. The reason David Whyte is so successful with poetry [in organizations] is because it takes you into this subterranean level of human experience."

Whyte, author of *The Heart Aroused*, uses poetry to reclaim the language and metaphors that are part of our broader human inheritance. People then can understand and come to grips with many of the dynamics with which they are confronted. He contends we underestimate the drama of the workplace:

"The inherited language in the work world is far too small for the kind of mythic drama that occurs there every day; we need a language commensurate with the drama of work. I do think that most companies are like Shakespeare's plays, written large with dramatic entrances and exits, midnight assassinations, noble speeches while the grave diggers are telling it as it is, and every epoch ends with a lot of blood on the floor."

If the art we confront is more complex and advanced than our social capacities, we have an opportunity for growth and transformation. Music, for example, has complexities beyond our capacities to perceive them. Pogacnik explains:

"Take for example the relatively simple 'Trio Sonata' by Bach. Three systems move in a complex way without losing their identity. If you are in a position to hear these three 'voices' moving in a contrapuntal way, individually and together as they relate to each other and unfold together in 5, 6, or 7 minutes, it is practically an impossible task. It is so difficult to be present in all that. That is what I mean by art being way ahead of our capacities."

Music can teach us to listen instantly and truly hear what is going on and not get stuck in conventions or patterns in which we usually operate—crucial skills in a business environment.

The arts take us on adventures in creative expression that help us explore safely unknown territory, overcome fear, and take risks. We can transfer these learning experiences to the workplace. Art-making has an alchemical effect on the imagination. Art takes people out of the realm of analytical thinking and into the realm of silence, reverie, and heightened awareness.

In my own work with organizations, I've noticed this shift in consciousness creates a crucible for deep conversation, from which emerges trust, caring, camaraderie, and genius-level thinking. A shared art experience enhances our sense of belonging and enriches conversation. Participants in my seminars have observed that:

"Art can be part of the process of bridging gaps/polarities."

"Art creates a different kind of conversation than the verbal/cerebral one of the workplace."

"Painting was an experience of listening with other senses."

"Art gives us new ways to experience each other."

Learning to Collaborate

Below are what some of today's leading management thinkers say about the arts and collaboration in organizations, beginning with business author Margaret Wheatley:

> "I think people naturally love to affiliate and prefer working together, but then we put them in organizations and in this highly competitive American culture where people learn to pit themselves against each other. But most people don't like that. When we're asking people to work together in teams and to care for each other, we're actually working with a natural energy. I mean it's the natural tendency of humans. In this particular Western, North American culture, we have so conditioned people to be competitive and to look out for themselves that teamwork has become a problem. Yet working together is a more natural state for humans than working in isolation, and teamwork is a natural tendency. The arts, and sports as well, provide people with the experience of what it's like to work together.
>
> If you're making beautiful music together, or making a powerful mural together, or doing drama together, it becomes instantly known to people that they couldn't have done this alone and that there's a real joy in working it through and all the difficulties of putting on a production of any kind, working together. All those difficulties just sort of melt away when you're in the actual performance or looking at what you've created together. That's an experience we certainly need more of in organizations, and I think that kind of experience with teamwork is available through the arts because it does call on our full humanity."

Dick Baumbusch, a marketing consultant who collaborates with Todd Siler, says when they gave a team of people "artistic tools" to communicate with, it put them on a level playing field and no one could manipulate or dominate the conversation: "The goal is to leverage and capitalize on the collective intelligence of the group, not to reflect what the boss wants to hear." Visual art activities make it easy for introverts to express themselves on an equal footing with extroverts and make it easier to discuss ideas without getting personal. This is because you discuss the thoughts expressed by the art, not the art (or the artist's effort) itself. Every idea expressed through the art has a chance to be seen and heard, rather than maintaining a focus on ideas emanating from those who are eloquent or domineering. As

Baumbusch points out, "This is critical because people who don't get heard can later sabotage the implementation process."

Reinforcing the power of using art to communicate, the CEO of ING said the organization condensed six months of strategic work into two days by using art as part of the process. Siler elaborates: "The arts help us see in every conceivable way the larger picture and mission we're trying to move toward." Art is essential to the conversation. Tim Merry, a musician and organizational transformation practitioner, notes, "People need to go places inside themselves they can't go if they just sit there and talk. And if you want to create some kind of sustainable change, you have to connect to people's passion. And this is what the arts do. They connect people's passion, and when you're playing music, for example, it's the great leveler. The boss has a clave and you have a bass drum. And once that level ground has been established, then really important conversations can take place."

Examples of the Arts as a Vehicle for Collaboration in Organizations

The Xerox PARC Artist-in-Residence Program

The Palo Alto Resource Center (PARC) Artist-in-Residence Program (PAIR) began at PARC in 1993 and remained active through 1999. As John Seely Brown, former director of PARC, explains:

> "The PAIR program invites artists who use new media into PARC and pairs them with researchers who often use the same media, though often in different contexts. The output of these pairings is both interesting art and new scientific innovations. The artists revitalize the atmosphere by bringing in new ideas, new ways of thinking, new modes of seeing, and new contexts for doing. This is radically different from most corporate support of the arts, where there is little intersection between the disciplines. It takes a bit of faith on both sides, and a belief that both science and art can use a little shaking up, to engage in such a partnership."

In his open letter to a young researcher, Seely Brown (*Harvard Business Review*, Jan/Feb 1991) describes the kind of spirit they expect in the research room at Xerox PARC:

> "At PARC, we attempt to pose and answer basic questions that can lead to fundamental breakthroughs. Our competitive advantage depends on our ability to invent radically new approaches to computing and its uses, and then bring these rapidly to market. If you come to work here, there will be no plotted path. The problems you work on will be the ones you help invent. . . . You will be challenged to take

risks and give up cherished methods or beliefs in order to find new approaches. You will encounter periods of deep uncertainty and frustration when it will seem that your efforts are leading nowhere. That's why following your instinct is so important. Only by having deep intuitions, being able to trust them, and knowing how to run with them will you be able to keep your bearings and guide yourself through uncharted territory. The ability to do research that gets to the root is what separates merely good researchers from world-class ones. The former are reacting to a predictable future; the latter are enacting a qualitatively new one."

This call to adventure has attracted the best talent in the world. John Seely Brown (JSB) pointed out to me (LN) a few other key elements of the PAIR program in our interview:

LN "In your PAIR program, do the artists and scientists also look at marketplace applications relative to what they're experimenting with, or inventing? Or doesn't that come into the conversation?"

JSB "That doesn't come into the conversation very much. Again, we expect our researchers to be incredibly familiar with the marketplace of whatever they happen to be doing. Our purpose is not to design products; our purpose is to create almost new ways of looking at the world, new industries, and so on. We were also striving to create a knowledge ecology within Xerox PARC."

LN "So it's an opportunity to carve out space and time for pure creativity and invention. Pure art—creativity and invention without worrying about consequences at that point?"

JSB "Right, although it's coupled with technical and scientific work at the same time. I mean we don't just sit there and build *anything*. What we were doing here was experimenting, for example, with fundamentally new genres. What might the newspaper of the future actually look like? What might be the way television and newspapers morph together? What would be both the artistic and human experience? That's just one example, but it was a very interesting consequence of the interplay between a couple of artists and some computer scientists."

LN "I do believe that there is an alchemical response to art when you put people together and you combine the art experience with the business talent."

JSB "Right. There are three ways I look at [the impact of an art experience]. One is the notion that engaging in these types of activities evokes deeper responses, deeper emotions. It brings forth many of the tacitly held beliefs and assumptions that you have. So think of it as evocative of the tacit knowledge. The second is that focused conversations are built and fused together around evocative objects that concern problems that the researcher has on his or her mind. I have said very often, it was the researcher who had the real problem, but the interaction with the artist actually made a big difference. Now that's a complex interplay, 'cause it takes over; it's like a conversation that unfolds over many months. The third concerns the power of simplicity. Simplicity prior to complexity doesn't mean much. But simplicity, after you pass through the wall of complexity, after you have marinated in a fully nuanced reading of the situation and then rendering it in very simple ways, is extraordinarily powerful."

LN "And you would have to have a capacity for chaos, too? That's the problem I think in most corporations. There's a fear, first of all, a fear of art, a fear of chaos, and a fear of losing control. Yet you were orchestrating all of this."

JSB "But out of that mixture, as long as you can provide the right gradient, the right field forces that cause things to grow in certain directions, like the sun 'pulling' plants in a certain direction—if you can honor the context—then you can produce great things collaboratively."*

Equiva Services: Art-Based Learning and Knowledge Creation

Equiva Services is the support services company for joint venture companies formed by Shell Oil Company, Texaco, and Saudi Refining (an affiliate of Saudi Aramco). Equiva Services provides services such as learning and development, human resources, information technology, and marketing. The joint venture companies were facing severe pressures to enter new markets with innovative products and delivery systems pertaining to downstream oil. Participants in a learning lab went out on field trips to study "new economy" companies to learn how they leverage creativity and high performance. Once they completed their information gathering, their next challenge was to synthesize their findings and make sense of it all.

Artist Todd Siler guided the group in making five-dimensional prototypes (sculptures) using his five dimensional (5-d) model-building process that incorporates (1d) words, (2d) images, (3d) structures, (4d) motions, and (5d) symbols. This process enabled participants to give form to their ideas and make unconscious (tacit) ideas conscious (explicit). Their artwork sparked inquiry, dialogue, storytelling, and reflection among the group. According to Nick Nissley and Gary Jusela, researchers involved in this project, these sculptures were the structural capital that "led to the telling of stories about how the energy of imagination and knowledge from the participants' field visits could be harnessed into intellectual capital."

---

* John Seely Brown is the former director of PARC and chief scientist of Xerox Corporation. He retired from Xerox in April 2002. PAIR is examined in detail in *Art and Innovation: The Xerox PARC Artist in Residence Program,* edited by Craig Harris and published by MIT Press.

Using art to visualize information and ideas is a simple and powerful way to make knowledge explicit. The art process made visible what it takes to operate in the new economy. According to Siler: "Using a wide range of disciplines in the arts, from sculpting, drawing, music, and literature to electronic arts, can really help people see their problems and opportunities differently. Art-making also helps people tap into their human potential, which every organization is founded on." He points out that if people talk about their ideas without visualizing them, it is easy to misinterpret what people mean:

> "You can have the best technology and the best position within a market, but if that human communication piece doesn't work it impacts on everything from the shareholders to the customers to the services rendered and delivered."**

LexisNexis: Improv in Corporate Training and Development***

"My own special area of focus is the performing arts and their applicability to corporate training and development. Teaching the soft skills by means of procedures 'bulletized' on PowerPoint charts can provide a framework, but the real challenge of utilizing those skills is to know how to fill in the spaces between the bullets or to know how to shift to another framework when the real world doesn't cooperate with bulleted procedures. Actors, especially improvisational actors, have been training their minds for centuries to deal with the unanticipated or, rather, to 'anticipate surprise.' All of the learnings of improvisational acting apply to learning soft skills in the workplace.

"At LexisNexis, it's very common for me to facilitate the work of a group of people who haven't worked together before and who often aren't located in the same city, country, or hemisphere. Their challenge can be equated to that of an improv team: To jointly create a coherent narrative from little more than, 'Here's the goal. Figure out how to get there.' Team members have to take that input and create [metaphorically] a long-form improv performance out of it, using the skills of the improvisational performer. They have to decide what their roles on the team are going to be. They have to really learn about true collaboration, which requires becoming comfortable with trusting one's instincts, with flexing one's reaction to follow the shift in the narrative, with supporting others and trusting them to support you. And all of their actions must be geared toward advancing the team

---

** Researchers Nick Nissley and Gary Jusela's study on Equiva was published in 2002 by ASTD.

*** From an interview with Jerry Kail, senior OD consultant, LexisNexis

toward a goal or, in improv terms, 'telling the story.' Team members must identify promising directions to follow, accept offers for exploration, relate all the various stimuli to the emerging narrative, strike out into risky areas, relinquish trying to control the ultimate outcome, and ultimately create a coherent result that incorporates as many of the threads as possible. In the best improv and the best business teams, there are no stars, no upstaging. The *team* is the star."

World Bank: Storytelling as a Catalyst for Collaboration****

"In 1996, while building the first knowledge management system at the World Bank, the subject-matter experts (SMEs) and the tech people hit a logjam because they did not understand each other's needs. I was designated to break the logjam.

"At my first session I brought a picture of my son, who was three months old at the time, and a replica of an Egyptian deity holding two worlds. I held up the picture of my son and said, 'I'm here because I know we are creating the world he is going to inherit. This is what gets me up in the morning. The World Bank has a mission in which it addresses many of the core issues of the world today and makes a difference. I feel deeply connected to our mission.'

"Then, I held up the replica: A king on bowed knees holding the two worlds. I shared that this was an ancient symbol of balancing multiple worlds. In our case we had to bridge the two worlds of content and technology. They could just as easily have been politics and mission or the spiritual and the mundane. I asked everyone to consider how they could hold both worlds, not letting go of either. I encouraged them to consider doing an excellent job of both delivering the content and developing the technology. The energy [of the group] shifted. The two symbols I used were personally meaningful to me and became touch points for the group. We moved to a higher level as collaborators because the caring component became explicit."

StorageTek: The Function of Art in Organizations*****

"There are standard practices that I use all the time: poetry and quotes in reports and emails; storytelling; video work that is far more than 'talking head'; role playing; using big drawing papers in meeting rooms for mind-mapping and vision sketching; skits for report-outs;

**** From an interview with Seth Kahan

***** From an interview with Lola Wilcox, senior OD consultant at StorageTek

fractal art; wet clay blocks and tools or the geometric shape toys to play with during particularly 'hot' meetings; visioning narration followed by sketching, et cetera.

"We also incorporate artists into conference space, particularly performance artists (from juggling to installation art); commission paintings for use in publication; provide musical instruments as walk-aways for conferences that people then use throughout the conference, building a "symphony" of collaboration; and use Playback Theater for power plant management teams' leadership culture change."

Why Use the Arts in Corporate Training?

According to Paul Smith, Arts and Business (UK):

"In an ASTD report titled 'Workplace Basics: The Essential Skills Employers Want,' seven groups of skills were listed:

1. Knowing how to learn
2. Reading, writing, and computation
3. Communication skills: speaking and listening effectively
4. Adaptability skills: solving problems and thinking creatively
5. Developmental skills: managing personal and professional growth
6. Group effectiveness: interpersonal skills, teamwork, and negotiation skills
7. Influencing skills: organizational effectiveness and leadership

"In part, this provides a clue to the effectiveness of arts-based development. If learning equals knowledge plus experience, then the most learned people are those who have breadth and depth of experience, and this is the key strength of the arts. Much of the focus of training activity is on bits of information or methods or some other kind of knowledge. But the arts are structured to create an experience. As a bonus, the experience that the arts create is often one which is more directly relevant to people and their behaviors and attitudes. Simply, the arts are better at quantifying and communicating the truly important ideas."

John Cimino, founder of Creative Leaps, says:

"Gregory Bateson, a seminal thinker in psychiatry, anthropology, and systems theory said that if you juxtapose two forms of description, such as art and science or art and business, that 'double description' affords you an unexpected bonus of insight akin to the perception of 'depth' in binocular vision—a surprise effect not predictable from working with either of the 'descriptions' alone. We all know that when we focus on something with just one eye, we see merely a monocular view. We are unable to perceive depth. Depth 'appears' when we use both our eyes at once. It is the same with our disciplines of knowledge. Each affords a discipline-based monocular view. For a more fully dimensional view, we need to juxtapose, and then integrate, the insights of several disciplines. The arts, I believe, are the ideal second descriptor, the ideal second lens for seeing into the depths of things. We develop, through art, thought-path legacies which become accessible to us no matter what we may be focusing on: life issues, global issues, business issues."

According to Gary Muszynski, musician and founder of One World Music:

"We can learn about collaborative processes (such as music and theater) that embrace paradox, helping us to become less fragmented. Music-making, for example, has been used for centuries as a way to bring the tribe and community together. I've always liked Max DuPree's observation that leadership needs to address two sides of organizational life: the scientific and the tribal. We need both in business today. And perhaps that is one of the central messages inherent in the arts. It is not either/or, but both/and. Certainly, jazz and improvisation [are] about embodying this central theme.

"Through music, we learn how to listen to others while still staying true to our own rhythms and melodies. We can learn about harmony and how to honor tension and allow it to feed the creative process. We can learn that every evolutionary process that occurs in organisms, organs, and organizations involves chaos and order working together as they do in the creative process. Finally, we can learn how to enliven and celebrate the human spirit instead of deadening it. That would be the greatest employee retention category imaginable."

Richard Olivier, founder of Mythodrama (UK), says:

"We work with theater techniques, poetry, and Shakespeare to improve presentation and leadership skills. An underlying theme for us is maximizing personal potential within an organizational context. We are often invited in when morale is low and people need a boost, whether it is a new strong competitor or internal dissension or new government legislation. We also work a lot with firms embarking on a major change initiative who need to engage both the hearts and the minds of their people. Every presentation, whether to a small team or a major conference, is a performance, and will achieve more impact if it is treated as such. It is particularly useful in emphasizing the difference between management and leadership. As leaders, people need to sell their vision, gather diverse others around a common goal, motivate their troops and paint positive pictures of the future—with words. Not a lot of engineers are taught this, but then suddenly they are promoted and are expected to do it."

Remarks Lena Bjørn, co-founder of The Decapo Theater (Denmark):

"We often work with companies in a period of transition. I think basically what we can do with the theater is to open up the dialogue. Maybe it has never been there; maybe it has been frozen for some reason. We activate their issues, but we do it in a safe way because we come with this fiction. Theatre can effect a kind of relief because we use a lot of humor—Ha-ha! Look at what they are doing. It's like us. So we can bring relief by being able to look at ourselves and we can bring reflection. How can we use the arts to create more effective learning experiences?"

Here's what Bob Root-Bernstein, professor of physiology at Michigan State University, says:

"Perhaps the most important way to improve the use of the arts in business is to recognize that the arts are not just a form of entertainment. Active participation in the arts trains minds, hands, and social skills. Learning and sharing an art form forces people to re-create the skills and the patterns and interactions that the most creative artists, musicians, playwrights, et cetera, invented in the past. Such re-creations bring together people within corporations who would otherwise never meet in the normal course of their professional work. New opportunities arise. Re-creation therefore leads to re-creation, which in turn fosters novel creation itself."

Says Paul Smith, director, Arts & Business (UK):

"Although there is often some nervousness about joining an arts-based development session, it is absolutely implicit that those sessions are something different, removed from the work environment, and that every participant is outside his or her normal zone. In other words, participants understand that it is all right (demanded?) that they take risks, but that it is very safe to do so. If one tries to teach a person to do a new job task that exposes a weakness in front of colleagues, anxiety and resistance will be high. But teach someone to juggle in a room full of colleagues also dropping balls, and people laugh and enjoy the shared experience.

"And the process can have direct business benefits. A very large grocery chain in the UK identified breakage among night stocking staff as a cost that could be reduced and decided to experiment by engaging a circus skills group to teach juggling skills to increase dexterity. What they discovered was that by investing in this normally ignored group of employees, the night staff felt better about the company, which drove up productivity and drove down pilfering. The company also discovered that much of the breakage was not due to clumsiness but boredom and that the workshops had given the employees a new interest in their work."

Debriefing an Arts Experience

Sivasailam "Thiagi" Thiagarajan offers the following thoughts about debriefing arts activities:

"One of the things I always do is to follow up an improv session with a systematic debriefing so when strong feelings come out, we go through a series of questions. If you are the manager, how would you deal with this? And if you are an employee, how would you deal with this? What would be the creative collaborative approach for you to take in this situation? So we do a lot of debriefing, talking about the feelings and the emotions and the anxieties and what should we be doing in situations.

"I use a simple six-step debriefing process. I ask:

1. How do you feel?
2. What did you learn?
3. What insights did you get?
4. How does this picture/short story/piece of drama relate to your work world?
5. If this art is a metaphor for something that's happening in the organization, what exactly does it portray? For example, in this picture, 'Who is the screaming child who ran away in the top left-hand corner and what would you do next, based on your insights?'
6. Have people draw their feelings and insights, exchange drawings, then use intuition to interpret and describe another person's drawing. [See Thiagi's activity, "Artistic Insights," in this book for detailed instructions.]

"It is important for the trainer or facilitator to keep in mind that these situations are not personal attacks, but a reaction to what has been hidden (in group dynamics or in the work environment). Sometimes it's important to be quiet. Don't solve the situation, and don't ignore their feelings. It IS important to let them process, vent, and gripe to get it out of their systems.

"One of the techniques I use is to make sure that art, whether it is painting or theater sports, things of that nature, brings out the hidden feelings, emotions, the skills and fantasies, things of that nature. However, if you are working with engineers, as I frequently do, you also need to relate what experiences they had to some kind of linear, left-brain type. I'm also very sensitive about how far I can push a group and when I should retreat. I make sure I don't make anyone appear foolish. I would rather have the group laugh at me rather than laugh at any of the participants."

Do Some Art Forms Work Better Than Others in Different Work Groups?

In answer, Jacquie Lowell, creativity and improv trainer (USA) says:

"Individuals have their own unique learning styles, and different art forms—or different exercises within a given art form—will appeal to different individuals according to these styles. I always tailor a training program to not only achieve the goals of the person who brings me into a company, but also to appeal to the population I will be working with. For example, introverts will generally prefer exercises they can do quietly at a table by themselves or with a single partner, using paper and pen or art materials. Extroverts will prefer group interactive exercises. Visual thinkers will prefer exercises involving art materials, kinesthetic thinkers will prefer exercises involving movement, and auditory thinkers will prefer music or conversation.

"My experience is that if participants feel safe, if they view the workshop as a laboratory for creative exploration rather than a performance situation, they will respond well to interesting exercises that are well outside their preferred modes."

Guidelines for Conducting an Arts Experience

Many of the people interviewed expressed concern about the arts being appropriated or trivialized if not conducted with authenticity, emotional safety, and respect. We offer the following guidelines for facilitators:

- It is important to practice art in some form yourself so that you have a visceral, experiential understanding of art-making and not just an intellectual understanding.

- When conducting a visual art activity, tell participants not to compare their work with others, but to focus on the process. The process is more important than the outcome.

- Ask participants to think and feel for themselves, to trust their own way of perceiving the world. This is key to genius-level thinking.

- Tell participants to be open and receptive to the new and unexpected.

- Make sure it is safe for people to express themselves and that everyone has a voice. Participants also should have a choice of not speaking.

- Remember to have fun and let the experience be one of adventure.

- Inspire courage in your group to try something new and to help them move from the known to the unknown and then back again.

David Pearl, pioneer of Experience Engineering™ (United Kingdom), offers this additional advice:

> "Treat everyone you work with as creative geniuses. The genius may or may not be fully recognized or expressed, but as facilitators you must know it is there. When you treat people as creative, that is how they behave.
>
> "Remember, you can't give what you don't have. Meaning, simply, whatever a business is trying to offer the world outside itself, it must also do inside itself."

As T.S. Eliot said, "We shall not cease from exploration. And the end of all our exploring will be to arrive where we started. And know the place for the first time."

3 Getting Acquainted and Icebreakers

Getting Acquainted
- Chairs
- More Than 1,000 Words
- Personality Typing
- Sing, Sing a Song

Icebreakers
- Belly Dancing
- Building Community
- Check In
- Inspiration Rituals

CHAIRS

Objectives

- To discover roles and patterns in teams
- To explore alternative ways of working together
- To become more comfortable working with the other participants

Uses

- Communication
- Team building
- Conflict
- Leadership
- Getting acquainted

Art Form

- Theater improvisation

Time Required

45 to 60 minutes

Materials, Handouts, and Equipment

- Colored, peel-off rectangular stickers, approximately 2" x 3" in size. There should be enough stickers to divide the participants into color-coded groups (for example, if there are three groups of five, provide five stickers each of three different colors).
- Markers
- One bell or whistle
- Chairs (twice as many as there are people)
- Written directions for each group (see Step 4)

Procedure

1. Place the chairs in the center of a large room.
2. Tell participants to select a colored sticker and apply it to their clothing or nametag. The color they select will be the color for their group. For example, if there are fifteen participants and you want three, five-person groups, there might be red, blue, and orange groups.
3. Ask each group to stand in different areas of the room.
4. Give each group separate written instructions on what to do during the activity:

    Group #1: Put all the chairs in the room by the window (or door if there are no windows).

    Group #2: Put all the chairs in the room in a circle.

    Group #3: Put all the chairs in the room by the far wall.

    If there are more than three groups, you will need to write some additional instructional sheets.

5. Inform everyone that the activity is about to start and that each group has 10 minutes to complete its instructions. Use a countdown to add some pressure and ring a bell or blow a whistle when they are to start.
6. After 10 minutes, stop the exercise and bring the group into a circle.
7. Place the stickers in a box in the center of the room. Have the participants focus on each sticker and release any tension into the sticker that remains from the activity.

Discussion

Use the following questions to guide a discussion:

- Did participants fight over the chairs? Why?
- What roles emerged if they fought over the chairs?
- Did participants compare instructions?
- Did some refuse to take part at all?
- What does such chaos, if any, reveal about people in groups?
- How evident was open communication and negotiation?
- What would have made the exercise easier? More difficult?

- What happened in the activity not already discussed?
- Where there any moments of particular tension? What did you feel at these times?

Contributor

Tim Merry is a partner in Engage! InterAct, an organization that encourages people to look to the benefits of difference and diversity and helps them work together to promote and celebrate the values of respect, cooperation, and creativity. Engage! InterAct works with youth, commercial, nonprofit, and governmental organizations.

MORE THAN 1,000 WORDS

Objectives

- To become acquainted with team members and group participants
- To build team spirit by learning about each other
- To demonstrate that people often have much in common

Uses

- As a fun get-acquainted activity (it is best slated first on the agenda)
- Team building that inspires creativity

Art Form

Collage

Time Required

Approximately 35 to 45 minutes

Materials, Handouts, and Equipment

For each team:

- One large foam core board (or mat board), approximately 20" x 30"
- Assortment of full-page images, pre-ripped from magazines; at least five pages per person. The images can be any picture, person, place, thing, symbol, color, or word from any advertisement or article. To ensure a variety of images, include magazines that cover a range of subjects (for example, travel, entertainment, technology, business, fashion, cooking, photography).
- Scissors, at least two pairs for every three people
- Scotch® tape and/or glue stick, at least two for every three people
- Two bold markers

Procedure

1. Instruct participants to form teams of four to eight people.
2. Provide each team one set of materials.

3. Explain that they will be making a team biograph—a pictorial resume that includes interesting professional and personal facts about each team member.

4. Ask each team to create a collage of magazine images (for example, any picture, person, place, thing, symbol, color, word, in whole or part) that symbolizes details about their backgrounds, skills, achievements, hobbies, interests, et cetera. For instance, someone from information systems who recently traveled to France might find pictures of a computer and the Eiffel Tower to include in the team biograph.

5. Tell participants that they may select any number of images. Each participant may also draw one additional item using a marker.

6. Remind everyone that this is a team activity. Therefore, participants must agree as a team to the final composition of their collages.

7. Inform participants that they will have about 20 minutes total to create their team biographs: about 10 to 15 minutes to find relevant images, plus 5 to 10 minutes to compose their collages. Give participants periodic time updates.

8. Ask each team to present its biograph to the entire group (that is, disclose which images are associated with which team members, describe why specific images were chosen and what they connote, tell how different images were integrated, and reveal why particular images appear more prominent).

Discussion

Lead a debriefing using the following questions:

- Were you surprised by the number of skills and hobbies shared within your team and across the group?

- What were some of the most unusual or most interesting facts you learned about someone?

- What did your team do that allowed you to work well together? How could you apply these principles to other work situations?

- Do you feel you established a team identity? Why or why not?

Contributor

Holly M. O'Neill is founder and principal of Talking Business, a marketing consultancy specializing in strategy, branding, marketing research, and product planning. By integrating creativity with structure, Talking Business delivers breakthrough concepts and solutions that optimize clients' marketing efforts and accelerate their visionary initiatives.

PERSONALITY TYPING

Objectives

- To help people gain insight into how they perceive themselves and others
- To access an individual's personality type

Uses

- A fast, unique way to identify personality types
- Ideas for interviewing
- Group formation
- Decision making

Time Required

20 to 30 minutes

Art Form

Music

Materials, Handouts, and Equipment

- A copy of the Interview Questions handout for each participant
- A copy of the Picture of Musical Instruments handout for each participant
- A copy of the Musical Instrument Personality Type handout for each participant
- Pens or pencils for participants

Procedure

1. Divide the participants into groups of two.
2. Distribute a copy of the Interview Questions handout and a pen or pencil to each participant.
3. Instruct participants to take turns interviewing each other as a detective would in order to gather the facts about a case. Have them use the handout for interview questions. They don't need to record their responses; however, they should make mental notes of their answers. Tell them that the interviews should last 5 minutes each and that it's not necessary to use all the questions on the handout.

4. Tell the participants to begin.

5. After 5 minutes, tell the pairs to switch roles.

6. After 5 more minutes, tell the participants to stop interviewing. Distribute a copy of the Pictures of Musical Instruments handouts and the Musical Instrument Personality Type handout to each participant.

7. Ask the participants to assess their partner's personality type by selecting an instrument that best describes that person's personality traits. To do this, have them look at the pictures of all the instruments to familiarize themselves with them. Then refer them to the Musical Instrument Personality Type handout.

8. Encourage each pair to try to come to agreement on which instrument best describes each person.

Discussion

Lead a discussion using the following questions:

- How accurate was the instrument type chosen for you?
- If the instrument type chosen to describe you was not accurate, in what way was it not?
- How accurate were you in choosing your partner's instrument? In what way?
- What combination of instrument types would be best for optimal team performance?
- How might you use a combination of musical instruments to improve team performance?

Contributor

Janice Kilgore has varied experiences in the professional music world as well as being a devout music educator and musician. She was trained at the University of North Texas with degrees in music education (B.M., M.M.E.). She is currently working on a doctorate at UNT in creative thinking through music education applications. She has served as a consultant and lecturer since 1987 and is in over ten editions of *Who's Who*, including *Who's Who in Entertainment*. Ms. Kilgore has created a distance learning music education program for children and contributed to several exercises in *101 Great Games and Activities* (Pfeiffer). She is currently on staff at Tarrant County College, Southeast Campus, as a music instructor.

Interview Questions

1. What is your favorite type of music?
2. Who is your favorite singer?
3. What is your dream job?
4. What is your favorite hobby?
5. What is your favorite color?
6. What is your favorite food?
7. Would you prefer to be a leader or follower?
8. What is your favorite automobile?
9. Are you an introvert or extrovert?
10. Are you a people watcher or someone who likes to be watched?
11. Do you like to cook or to be served?
12. What is your favorite vacation spot?
13. Are you a lover or a warrior?
14. Are you a risk taker or do you play things safe?
15. Are you a homebody or a world traveler?
16. Are you single-minded or a multitasker?
17. Do you consider yourself to be loud or quiet in nature?
18. Are you pushy or someone who gets pushed around?
19. Are you a "know-it-all" or are you someone who asks a lot of questions?
20. Are you sweet or sassy?

Reproduced from *Orchestrating Collaboration at Work* by Arthur B. VanGundy & Linda Naiman with permission of the publisher. Copyright © 2005 by Arthur B. VanGundy & Linda Naiman.

Pictures of Musical Instruments

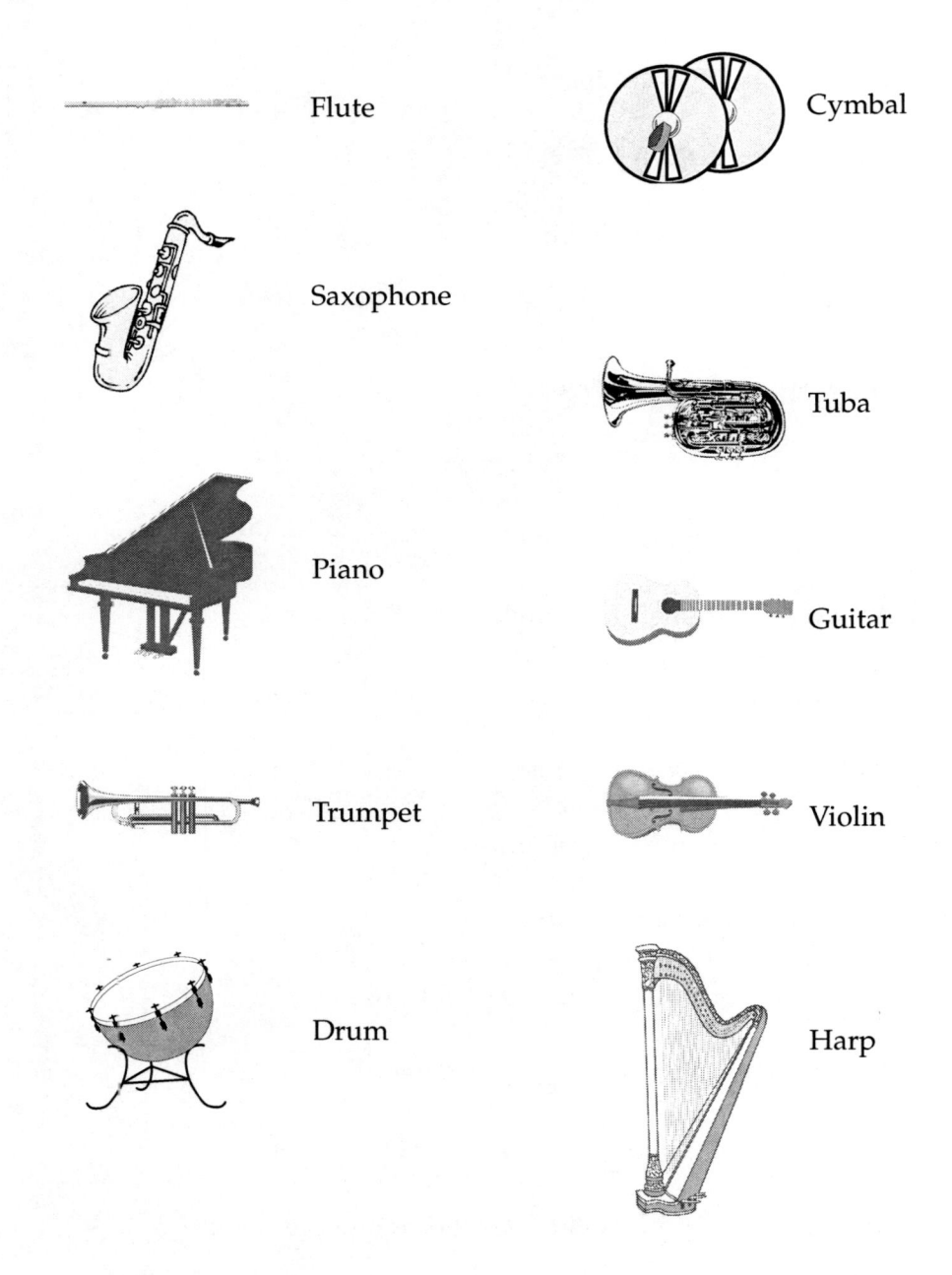

Flute

Cymbal

Saxophone

Tuba

Piano

Guitar

Trumpet

Violin

Drum

Harp

Reproduced from *Orchestrating Collaboration at Work* by Arthur B. VanGundy & Linda Naiman with permission of the publisher. Copyright © 2003 by John Wiley & Sons, Inc.

Musical Instrument Personality Type

Flute—quiet, sweet personality, introvert

Saxophone—jazzy personality, risk taker, extrovert

Piano—multitasking abilities, jack-of-all-trades, sees things with a global perspective

Trumpet—brash, impulsive, strong leadership qualities

Drum—a pacesetter, bombastic but sassy

Cymbal—scintillating, flamboyant, zest for life

Tuba—teddy-bearish, fun and lovable

Guitar—passive, goes with the flow, laid back

Violin—prima donna, has to have everything his or her way, knows own mind

Harp—know-it-all, but angelic

SING, SING A SONG

Objectives

- To create ownership of group tasks
- To develop and sustain group identity

Uses

- Getting acquainted
- Small group warm-up
- Group energizer
- Team building in newly formed groups

Art Form

Music ensemble

Time Required

20 to 30 minutes

Materials, Handouts, and Equipment

- One 3" x 5" index card for each participant, prepared as in Step 1

Procedure

1. Prior to the activity, write the name of one song on each card corresponding to the number of groups and people within the groups. For instance, to form three groups with four people in each group, you would use three different songs and write each song name on four cards. If you need more than four groups for your next activity or to make the groups smaller when you have a large audience, include more tune titles. Sample tunes include "Three Blind Mice" "Row, Row, Row Your Boat," "London Bridge," "Old MacDonald," "If You're Happy and You Know It," "Ring Around the Rosy," "Skip to My Lou," "Oh, Susanna," "Camptown Races," "Yankee Doodle," "Mary Had a Little Lamb," "Jingle Bells," "Twinkle, Twinkle, Little Star," and "Happy Birthday." (For additional songs, use easy-to-sing, non-religious, non-political songs.)

2. Distribute the cards randomly as participants enter the room.

3. Tell the audience that the purpose of this activity is to form groups. To do so, they are going to sing the tunes written on their cards.

4. Have them sing their tunes in their minds as a warm-up activity.

5. Tell the participants to sing their songs aloud while walking around and continue singing aloud until they find others singing the same song. Encourage the singers not to be intimidated or inhibited by singing since no one is judging their voices and everyone is participating.

6. Once two members locate each other, tell this ensemble to continue roving as "wandering minstrels" to find others with the same tunes. (They could also stake out a claim in a selected portion of the room and allow the remaining members to find them.)

7. Instruct the singers to repeat the melody until all members of each group are found and there are no more searchers from the larger audience.

Discussion

Advise the participants that, even though from a distance the cacophony of the sound texture may seem unintelligible, the individual sounds of the group bring order. Note that Charles Ives, the composer, did this very same thing in his compositions. The result was a rich texture of sounds that, at first hearing, sounds like a wall of sound with no distinct parts. After closer listening, the individual tunes paint a tapestry of his musical themes.

Use the following questions to guide the discussion:

- Did you find the sounds to be unintelligible when you first began the activity?

- As you found another member of your group, were you better able to focus on your melody and block out the other melodies floating through the air?

- As you gained more members of your group, did you feel a sense of camaraderie? Why or why not?

- Did the song unite you and your teammates after the group finally was together?

- Do you think this activity will result in stronger team member bonds when it is used, in contrast to just grouping people randomly or by counting off?

Contributor

Janice Kilgore has varied experiences in the professional music world as well as being a devout music educator and musician. She was trained at the University of North Texas with degrees in music education (B.M., M.M.E.). She is currently working on a doctorate at UNT in creative thinking through music education applications. She has served as a consultant and lecturer since 1987 and is in over ten editions of *Who's Who,* including *Who's Who in Entertainment.* Ms. Kilgore has created a distance learning music education program for children and contributed to several exercises in *101 Great Games and Activities* (Pfeiffer). She is currently on staff at Tarrant County College, Southeast Campus, as a music instructor.

BELLY DANCING

Objectives

- To energize through movement
- To provide humor and entertainment for participants
- To provoke discussion on differences in personality and how they relate to movement

Uses

- A transition from one activity to another
- A mid-afternoon energizer
- A warm-up exercise

Art Form

Dance

Time Required

Approximately 5 minutes

Materials, Handouts, and Equipment

- A portable stereo
- Middle Eastern dance music (check copyright restrictions)

Procedure

1. Tell participants:

   "This is a quick energizer/personality test taken from Middle Eastern dance, also known as belly dance. Its ancient origins are the folk dances that celebrate nature. They also were intended to tell a story about the inner nature of people in general and the dancer in particular. We will try three basic, easy movements in this dance form that represent three aspects of the natural world and of human nature. As we go through each movement, pick which one you feel most connected to today."

2. Have everyone stand up and follow along with your movements.

3. Tell them that the first movement is with the head. Have them raise their arms, create a bow shape above their heads, and move their heads from side to side.

4. For the second movement, tell participants to stretch their arms out to either side and wave them and to move their hips from side to side.

5. Next, lead them through the third movement, the "shimmy," which consists of quick hip movements back and forth.

6. Ask: "Who feels most connected to the first movement? If so, do it with me. You are the sun people—visionary leaders who can see the big picture. A successful career is easy for you."

7. Ask: "Who feels most connected to the second movement? Do it with me. You are the ocean people. Warm and compassionate with great emotional intelligence. A successful relationship is easy for you."

8. Ask: "Who feels most connected to the third movement, the shimmy? You are the earth people: grounded, detail-oriented, and rooted in your values. It is said that for you a successful home life is easy."

Discussion

Lead a short discussion asking such things as:

- How did the movement description relate to your personality type?
- What did the movements chosen by others tell you?
- How do you feel since doing those movements?
- How can dance and movement help you understand yourself or others better?
- What did you learn that might improve collaboration within your team?

Contributor

Carla Rieger, B.A., C.R.P., is a performance storyteller, trainer, and humorist. She specializes in using theater, storytelling, and humor to enhance communication within diverse groups. She has over fifteen years of experience in dance, acting, comedy, and playwriting. She is the director of YES Education Systems, a creative communications consulting firm, and is the co-founder of the Vancouver Playback Theatre Troupe. She is currently touring her latest solo show, Dancing Between Worlds, that explores the perilous journey of reclaiming one's creative self. Her two manuals, *The Power of Laughter* and *Captivate Your Audience,* promote the use of fun and play in workplace settings. Her work has been featured on radio, TV, and in magazines. As a frequent speaker and performer before all types of business and civic groups internationally, Rieger helps build bridges both inside and out.

BUILDING COMMUNITY

Objectives

- Increase rapport among team participants
- Build an environment of openness and collaboration

Uses

- Icebreaker
- Sets the tone for a productive retreat or workshop
- Introduces people to each other outside of their work roles and relationships
- Sets the stage for exploring corporate responsibility

Art Form

Storytelling

Time Required

20 minutes for ten people; 60 minutes for forty people

Materials, Handouts, and Equipment

- A natural object (for example, a rock) or hand-crafted item that is easy to pass among participants.
- A musical instrument that makes a single tone, such as a Nepalese bowl gong. However, any musical interlude that is meditative will do.

Procedure

1. Recite the following background information and instructions:

    "For thousands of years people have come together to share their stories, listen, and learn about each other. It is a natural way of being together and provides insights into who we are, how we work together, and what we have to offer each other. I would like to share a poem and then hear your authentic response to it. I am more interested in hearing about your response to the poem than

I am in what the poem says. I have chosen this poem because it elevates the context of our discussion, but it is not necessary for you to agree with or enjoy the poem for us to have a productive discussion. It is most important that you are honest and your response is heartfelt. I am asking you to listen to a poem, not analyze a position. Please allow yourself to freely associate as the words run over you. You may find that your response is not rational; that is perfectly fine."

2. Show the natural object you brought to the group.

3. Continue with the following instructions:

"We will use this rock as a symbol. Because it occurs in the natural world and it doesn't need any justification, the rock will be our symbol of sharing truth; truth with a little 't,' not a big 'T.' I am looking for individual truth, the kind that comes simply from speaking honestly about your experience. When the rock comes your way, you may choose to share. It's also okay to pass, not saying anything. And it's okay to speak on an unrelated topic if that's what you have to say. Finally, it's okay to just hold the rock in silence. Does anyone have any questions, comments, or concerns?"

4. Ask participants to close their eyes or look down at the floor as they listen to the words of the poem. Then strike the Nepalese bowl gong and recite the following poem clearly and in an unhurried pace. Then say:

"If time was not an obstacle and we could invite all of our ancestors to be here, present with us, what would they tell us? If our grandparents . . . and their parents . . . could be here, what would they have to say about our work in the world? And if the ancestors of other species could be here: eagles, elephants, snakes, and fish . . . the mountains that are now dust, the clouds that have become part of the sea, the rivers that are now dry . . . what messages would they have for us and how we live our lives? Hear me, ancestors, you are not trapped by the narrow views we hold, by the constraints we place on ourselves and the politics of our workplace. . . . What do you have to tell us here, today, about what we have to offer the world?" [pause again and stike the gong]

"If time were not an obstacle and we could invite all of the children yet to be born here with us now, what would they tell us? If we invited the children yet to be born of all species: the caribou and antelope, the coral snake, the currents not yet formed deep in oceans, the clouds not yet assembled, and the winds not yet blown . . . and our own children . . . and their children . . . and their children . . . . Hear me, children yet to be born, help us remember that the world we are building is the world you will inherit. Help us to create a world worthy of your spirit." [strike gong and pause]

"If space were not an obstacle and we could invite all beings in the world to be here, present with us now, what could we do together? If the bushes that line our streets, the clouds that fill our skies, the mountains on the horizon, the great seas and rivers, the ravens, the elephants, the mountain lions, and the salamanders, the strangers on the other side of the world, and our own children, partners, lovers, friends, and colleagues could all gather together . . . could we lean on each other, learn from each other, and move forward together? What could we . . . would we . . . do?" [Gonggg . . . long pause]

5. Offer the rock to open the sharing. Listen. Allow gaps of silence to be. Do not underestimate the power of silence in helping the group to form or allowing participants to deepen their responses. Model attentive listening and respect. Only intervene if one person is clearly taking so much time that others will not have time to share.

6. When the sharing is complete, thank the participants and put away the rock. It is helpful to make some encouraging comments regarding the quality of the sharing that took place to further encourage increased authenticity as you go on to the next point in the agenda.

Discussion

Lead a brief discussion using the following questions:

- How did you experience this exercise in general?

- Were you comfortable, uncomfortable, bored, totally immersed, confused?

- After listening to the poem, what do you think your ancestors, children, or other living beings could tell you about yourself? About improving team collaboration?

- How useful would this exercise be prior to more focused, team-building exercises?

Reference

The poem above is a modified version from *World as Lover, World as Self* by Joanna Macy (Parrallax Press, 1991).

Contributor

Seth Kahan helps organizations and individuals improve performance. As a keynote speaker, he has addressed thousands. As a consultant, he has delivered global institutional change initiatives that rely heavily on employee cooperation for success. He works with senior management as a "social architect" building institutional community to accomplish strategic objectives.

CHECK IN*

Objectives

- To build community and create trust
- To foster empathic listening, spontaneity, intuition, and creativity
- To hone communication skills for non-verbal expression and comprehension

Uses

- Icebreaker
- Getting acquainted
- Team building

Art Form

Theater improvisation

Time Required

Approximately 30 minutes

Materials, Handouts, and Equipment

- A bell or chime

Procedure

1. Ask participants to stand in circles of no more than ten people, with no furniture between them. The room should be large enough to accommodate participants' circles, so each person in a circle has ample room to move. Chairs and other furniture can be moved to the outer edges of the room to maximize available space.

2. State the objectives of the activity, then describe and demonstrate the exercise with a small group of volunteers.

---

* Note: This activity comes from the Playback Theatre tradition. Playback Theatre is an interactive, improvisational structure based on honoring the audience's stories as a way to build community and celebrate the universality of our experience. Playback Theatre was developed in 1975 by The Original Playback Theatre Company under the direction of Jonathan Fox.

3. Invite everyone to take a minute to "check in" with how he or she is feeling—physically, mentally, emotionally.

4. After a moment to reflect, invite each person to create a sound and gesture that represents how he or she is feeling. The expression is generally fairly brief—using only one or two breaths. Demonstrate a sound or gesture they might use, such as a loud sigh while wiping their hands across their foreheads.

5. Tell the other members of their circle to simultaneously repeat the sound and movement immediately after each person presents his or her sound and movement. Continue in a call and response rhythm until each person in the circle has "checked in" and been mirrored by the group.

   (*Note:* When inviting participants to express themselves in what may be new or unfamiliar ways, encourage them to be willing to dive in and go with their first impulse. Using sounds instead of language offers the opportunity to be playful; movement may be subtle or broad. Seek to elicit an authentic expression for each individual's experience. When responding to each call, the intent is to honor the other person's experience and reflect it back with respect and acknowledgment.)

6. Tell participants to focus on playing back the essence of the expression, rather than worrying about replicating exactly the other's sound and gesture. In addition, individuals responding may make any adjustments needed to respect their own physical limitations, flexibility, et cetera. For example, if the "check-in" involves a somersault, an individual responding might opt to crouch over and roll his or her hands in a gesture that suggests the somersault.

Discussion

Invite participants to share reflections, first in pairs or within their circles and then with the whole group. Questions that can guide the reflection and application include the following:

- What did you notice?

- How is it useful?

- Were you aware of censoring your expression?

- What was it like to see your expression played back for you?

- How did it feel to "step into the other person's shoes" for an instant?

- Did you find it freeing to express yourself without words? Why or why not?

- What do you think you know about the group that you didn't know prior to checking in?

- In everyday interactions, how might your perception or echoing of gestures enhance empathy and communication?

Variations

1. In order to create a safe environment for exploration and risk taking when offering experiential exercises, preface the work with the following guidelines:

    - Remind participants that they possess free will and all participation is voluntary. They can choose to witness any exercise the group will explore.

    - Remind them you are intentionally choosing activities that will bring a fresh perspective and create new avenues of learning, which may, by their very nature, seem unfamiliar or unusual.

    - Ask participants to notice whether an activity feels uncomfortable. Encourage them to acknowledge their discomfort and to stretch themselves—to expand beyond that limitation—by exploring *with* the group.

    - To demonstrate the above, invite people to sit or stand comfortably. Then have them raise their arms gently above their heads and notice how it feels. Then invite them to reach their arms as high as they can, stretch toward the ceiling, and notice if that feels different. For some, the stretching sensation may feel pleasurable; for some it may feel less comfortable than with arms merely raised or with arms at their sides, but in general it is unlikely anyone will report that it is actually painful.

        Discuss this distinction between sensation and pain—noting again that part of the experiential work may generate sensation (which may be perceived as "out of one's comfort zone"), but it is not intended or likely to create pain.

        With the above distinction in mind, again invite the group to explore the exercises, and their responses to them, with curiosity and be willing to stretch.

2. Another way to create a safe environment for this exercise is to encourage the group to use sound and movement to express an emotion or idea. The whole group can practice creating sounds and gestures, each offering his or her individual expressions simultaneously. For this warm up, have participants gather in small groups or disperse throughout the room.

- Direct everyone to spontaneously create a sound and movement in response to various suggestions. The expressions will be brief—the duration of only one breath. Thus, the direction can be: "At the sound of the bell, create a sound and movement in response to the word 'satisfied.'"[You may want to use other words or images than those suggested here.] Ring the bell and have all respond.

- Next, say, "At the sound of the next bell, create a sound and gesture in response to the word 'frustrated.'" Ring the bell and have all respond.

- Next, say, "Create a sound and movement in response to the word 'tired.'" Ring the bell and have all respond.

This cycle can be repeated any number of times. Try to create a spontaneous emotional expression, and encourage everyone to go with out the first thing that occurs to him or her. Offering the directions one right after the other helps to minimize censoring or thinking too much about what to do; responding all at once lessens the pressure of being watched.

3. In this variation of the "Check In" exercise, the "Call and Response" begins by inviting members to verbally check in by *briefly* answering a specific question in one or two sentences. Choose a question for the group, such as "How are you feeling?" "What have you just come from?" (hellish traffic, a relaxing weekend, a productive meeting) or simply, "What's up?" The call and response rhythm remains as the basic structure.

4. In this variation, the "call" (each participant's response to the question) is now verbal. Have the rest of the circle members simultaneously create their own individual sounds and gestures in response to each call. Here again, the intent is to honor the other person's experience and to reflect it back with empathy and respect. Tell each person to speak and then receive the group response until everyone in the circle has checked in.

5. This variation is also based on using the call as a verbal answer to a chosen question.

    - Before each person in the circle speaks, have him or her choose someone opposite in the circle, to whom he or she briefly describes a feeling or state of mind.

    - Tell the chosen person and the two people standing on either side of that person to create the "response" through sound and gesture.

- Instruct the three members of the circle to simultaneously offer their own individual sounds and movements spontaneously and to play back the essence of the "teller's" experience collectively. Again, it is vital to remember the intent is to honor the other person's experience and reflect it back with empathy and respect.
- Invite each person to check in and receive a response until everyone in the circle is acknowledged.

Contributor

Nan Crawford & Co. provides experiential training and presentations. Crawford's work ignites creativity, confidence, and clarity—catalyzing breakthroughs in leadership, communication, collaboration, and performance. She holds an MA in organization development and is the artistic director of Pacific Playback Theatre. Clients include *Fast Company*, IBM, Lucent, More Than Money, Target, and Office Depot.

INSPIRATION RITUALS

Objectives

- To set stage to make the shift to creative focus
- To stimulate and prepare for creative work and play

Uses

- Icebreaker
- Any situation that requires the full creative engagement of participants

Art Form

Theater improvisation

Time Required

20 to 30 minutes

Materials, Handouts, and Equipment

- One bag of small agates (available at gardening stores) or smooth, black river stones
- Soft meditative background music (check on copyright issues)

Procedure

1. Organize participants into small groups of four to seven people and read the following:

   "This process is much like the anchoring used by all athletes and performers. Before they step onto the stage or into the ring or crouch at the starting line, they use an internalized ritual to shift their focus to the task before them. In this instance, we are building and imprinting a specific neuro-circuit (with sensory detail and emotion) that can be evoked whenever you wish to move to a creative state."

2. Place the stones on a table and have each individual select his or her own special stone.

3. Have participants return to their seats and assume comfortable positions with their feet placed firmly on the floor, their bottoms comfortably supported by their chairs, and their backs straight.

4. Begin playing the quiet background music and ask people to hold their stones in their non-dominant hand and to close their eyes.

5. Guide the group members to place their attention at their nostrils and have them follow their breath in through their right nostril and out through their left one. They should do this three times. Then have them follow their breath in through their left nostril and out through their right three times and through both nostrils in and out three times.

6. Tell them to relax into the support of their chair. They should just lean back and allow their chairs to support them.

7. Ask them to go on an inner journey to find a perfectly safe, peaceful, and inspirational place, a place that is special and sacred to them. Have them notice, with as much sensory detail as possible, the qualities of this place (for example, How does it look? How does it feel? What can they smell there? What, if any, colors are there? What is the quality of the air and light? What is the temperature? What sort of textures are there?).

8. Tell them to just notice these things without judging and let it all be exactly as it is. Have them rest in this place and soak up the feeling of comfort and extraordinary inspiration there.

9. Have them look in their mind's eye around the place and find something that symbolizes the powerful nature of the place.

10. Once they have identified this symbol, have them feel the stones in their non-dominant hands and imagine this symbol being infused into the stone. Have them feel the very essence of their sacred space being transferred into their stones.

11. Ask them to recall a time from their past in which they experienced a feeling of inspiration. It can be from any time in their lives. It doesn't matter what the activity was or what caused the feeling. Just direct them to bring it to mind and feel that inspirational energy. Maybe they were inspired by a speech, a piece of music, a film, or a book.

12. Have them notice how it feels in their bodies. Notice how it makes them want to do something extraordinary with their energy, something creative, something new or different from how they usually do things. If they have other inspirational moments, they can also bring these to the foreground and feel them as well.

13. Have them notice every subtle nuance of the feeling of inspiration in their systems. Direct them to feel it from the bottoms of their feet to the top of their heads and feel its pulse flowing throughout their bodies. Have them build that inspirational energy in their body until they are almost ready to burst!

14. When that feeling is at its peak, have them rub the stones in their hands. Have them mix their inspirational energy with the power of their sacred spaces. Have them build the energy and rub it into their stones three times.

15. Tell them that whenever they need creative inspiration, all they have to do is pick up and rub their stones. This feeling then will return and prepare them for creative action.

16. Gradually bring them back from their experience and ask them to stretch. Remind them that whenever they need to do creative inspiration, they can pick up their stones and rub them. Have them also come up with a plan for where they will keep their stones and how they will use them before doing creative work.

Discussion

Guide a discussion with the following questions:

- How easy was it for you to relax during the exercise?
- If you had trouble relaxing, what do you think was the reason?
- Did you experience difficulties with the visualizations? Why or why not?
- Were you aware of the repetition and emotion involved in the exercise?
- How might this exercise apply to team collaboration?
- How much repetition of thought and deed do teams require until they can collaborate effectively?
- What rituals do you and your team use? How can you improve them?

Contributor

Gael McCool, Ph.D., is a behavioral consultant and teacher in the Vancouver area. In her active practice, McCool has provided consultation and training to such companies as the Walt Disney Company, Johnson & Johnson, and several television networks. She is currently on sabbatical writing her book, *Emotional Accountability*.

4 Arts Warm-Up Activities

- Abstraction and Composition
- Art Gallery
- Arts Expedition
- Express Yourself
- If Your Face Were a Poem
- Restrictions and Limitations
- Strike Up the Band
- Thinking Symbolically
- Transparency

ABSTRACTION AND COMPOSITION

Objectives

- To provide a foundation for using the arts
- To overcome fear of art
- To get creative juices flowing
- To experiment with form

Uses

- Warm-ups
- Creative thinking

Art Forms

- Painting
- Collage

Time Required

40 minutes

Materials, Handouts, and Equipment

For each participant:

- Black ink
- Brushes
- Containers for ink and water, or pencils (soft lead, such as 4B)
- Bond paper
- Scissors
- Still-life ingredients (for example, a vase of flowers with a bowl of fruit and a bottle of wine) or a photograph of a still life or landscape enlarged so everyone can see it. If you use a photograph, make a color copy for each participant.
- Abstraction and Composition Handout (for Variation)

Procedure

1. Place the art materials, still life ingredients, and handout on tables for each group of four to five participants.

2. Show the participants an example of a still life (or display a poster of a still life).

3. Read the following advice from Winslow Homer:

   "You must not paint everything you see, you must wait, and wait patiently until the exceptional, the wonderful effect or aspect comes. Then if you have sense enough to see it, well, that is all there is to that."

4. Say the following to participants:

   "Throughout the history of art, there have been only short periods of time when art movements focused on the exact representation of nature. In a sense, all art is abstraction in that we cannot duplicate nature; we can only respond and interpret it. The most challenging aspect of drawing and painting is learning how to see."

5. Ask the participants to examine the still life (or photograph) and analyze it using the following questions:

   - How is it composed?
   - Is the picture primarily vertical, horizontal, or diagonal?
   - What basic shapes make up the picture?
   - How is space created?
   - If you are looking at a photograph in color, what contrasts in color and shape can you see by squinting?

6. Instruct the participants to break down their still life or photograph into its simplest forms. (Cezanne, for example, saw nature as variations of the circle, square, and cylinder.) To do this, have them draw those forms using black, white, and shades of gray to reconstruct their pictures as abstract compositions.

7. Tell them to cut out the shapes they have made and rearrange them to create a new composition so that one key element is visually interesting to them.

Discussion

Suggest that the participants look at each other's pictures and share their thoughts and feelings about experimenting with abstraction and composition. Use the following questions to guide this discussion:

- What have you learned from this exercise?
- How can you apply the principles of abstraction to your work in general? To your team?
- What contrasts have you created? How do they contribute to your composition?
- What can you learn from the principles of composition that you can apply to your work?

Variation

Tell participants to focus on composition. A good composition involves contrasts in scale, shape, line, color or tone, and the figure/ground relationship. These contrasts create tension between the positive and negative space, dark and light, passive and active elements.

Distribute the Abstraction and Composition handout and refer to it as a reference for exploring composition and abstraction.

Have the participants draw five rectangles on one sheet of paper and create five new compositions using a single subject. While these drawings don't have to be purely abstract, they should be kept simple.

Ask them to discuss with a partner which ones are the most interesting and why.

Contributor

Linda Naiman, BFA, works with organizations to awaken genius-level thinking through the art and science of applying creativity, innovation, and visionary thinking to business strategy. Naiman is a life-long artist and presents workshops on creativity and innovation in North America and Europe.

Abstraction and Composition Handout

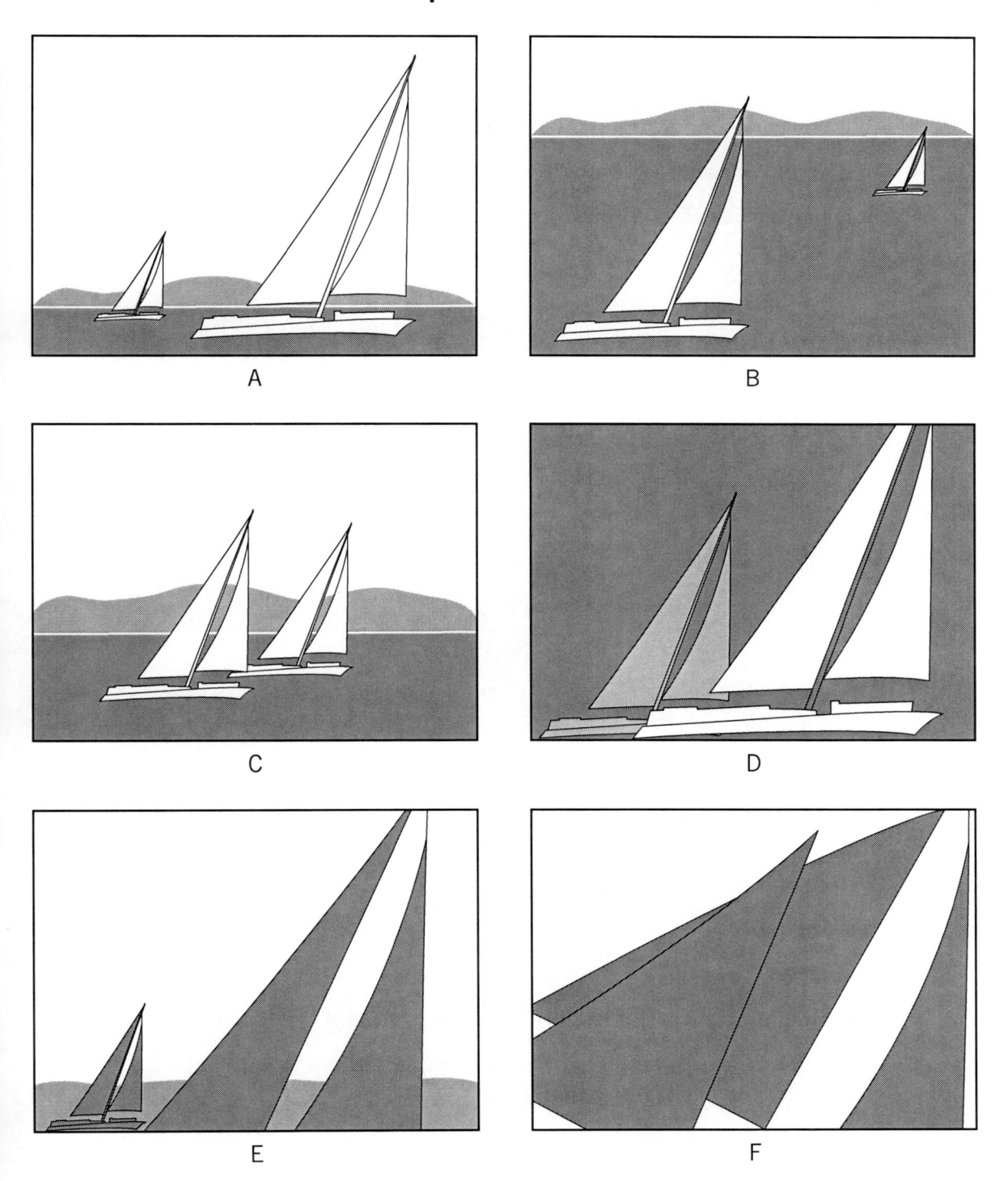

A

B

C

D

E

F

ART GALLERY

Objectives

- To identify desired training outcomes
- To help participants focus on desired training outcomes
- To create a consensus definition of classroom success

Uses

- Participant introductions
- Energizer
- Warm-up before a team-building session

Art Forms

- Drawing
- Music

Time Required

30 to 45 minutes

Materials, Handouts, and Equipment

- Colored markers or other drawing utensils
- A piece of drawing paper for each participant
- Masking tape
- CD player
- Visioning music CDs (for example, slow Mozart and Debussy)
- Drawing music (up-tempo light Mozart or light jazz—be sure not to violate any copyright restrictions)

Procedure

1. Begin playing the visioning music. Invite the participants to close their eyes and relax.

2. Lead them through muscle relaxation exercises—tightening and loosening muscles in their legs, arms, shoulders, neck, arms, and hands.

3. Ask the participants to visualize some team collaboration results they expect to achieve from the training. Suggest examples, such as seeing themselves communicating more productively with a difficult co-worker or celebrating with their team after completing a challenging project.

4. Once they have pictured their results, invite them to open their eyes and draw those results.

5. Begin playing the drawing music.

6. After about 5 to 10 minutes, ask them to post their drawings. (If a participant does not wish to post a drawing, honor that desire.)

7. Invite all to view the art gallery.

8. Lead a discussion about each drawing and ask each artist to discuss his or her work.

9. Invite any participants who did not post their drawings to share the outcomes they envision. (Do not ask them to display their artwork.)

10. Thank all the participants and lead a round of applause.

11. At the end of the session, return to the art gallery and use it as a framework for reviewing the day's learning.

Discussion

The following questions can be used to help guide a discussion after this activity:

- What did you learn about your expectations? Were they met? Why or why not?
- What did you learn about others' expectations?
- Are you more focused on your learning needs now?
- What should individuals do to improve team collaboration?
- Do you think that individual and team expectations are similar? Why or why not?
- How can you help each other reach desired team outcomes?

Contributor

Lenn Millbower is the author of *Training with a Beat, Cartoons for Trainers, Show Biz Training,* and *Game Show Themes for Trainers.* He is a magician, a music arranger, a pianist, an instructional designer, and an educator who combines entertainment and learning into interventions that are creative, meaningful, and fun.

ARTS EXPEDITION

Objectives

- To provide an introduction to arts principles
- To experience how the arts can enhance group idea generation
- To make connections between unrelated stimuli to enhance creativity

Uses

- Warm-up
- Creative thinking
- Communication

Art Form

Mixed media

Time Required

2 hours to one day

Materials, Handouts, and Equipment

One copy of the following for each participant:

- Spiral-bound notebook
- Pen or pencil
- A copy of the How to Look at Art handout
- A copy of the Arts Principles handout

Procedure

1. Prior to the session, select a local art museum or gallery with high-quality art. Request a tour or permission for a small group of three to fifteen participants to visit and schedule a date and time with the participants.

2. Ask the group of three to fifteen people to select a work-related challenge that needs an infusion of fresh ideas. Once they select a challenge, ask them to "put it on the back burner," that is, avoid concentrating on it until told to do otherwise.

3. Tell them they are going to look for clues on an arts expedition by making connections between what they see and experience on the expedition and the challenge they are working on.

4. Read the following aloud to the participants:

   "Priming the canvass in painting involves applying gesso (or another medium) as a ground before applying paint. In this activity, you are being primed to prepare yourself for the full spectrum of what the arts have to offer as a learning experience. According to Steve Zades (CEO of ad agency Long Haymes Carr), 'Contemporary art is the R&D lab of the future.' Zades takes staff and clients on expeditions to New York City to experience leading-edge art exhibits, groundbreaking theater, and trendy neighborhoods. The purpose of these expeditions is to 'tap into something that's on its way in, rather than already passed.'" (*Fast Company*, October 1999)

5. At the museum or gallery, distribute copies of the Arts Principles handout and the How to Look at Art handout and ask the participants to respond to the questions on the How to Look at Art handout for one or two pieces of art of their choosing. Tell them that, for the purpose of this exercise, art can be in any medium: painting, sculpture, video, new media, or conceptual.

6. Instruct the participants to write down any additional observations, ideas, or reactions they might have to the art as they proceed on their expedition.

7. Find a place to sit and compare notes. Have the group review the challenges they chose earlier and use their art experience to generate new ideas. Ask each person to share one of his or her observations from the notebook and have the group use the ideas as a stimulus to trigger ideas for the group challenge. Repeat this process until everyone has contributed at least one observation.

Discussion

Use the following questions to lead a discussion:

- What have you learned from this arts experience?
- What makes art a compelling experience?
- What did you find annoying?
- What trends do you see in our culture that have been influenced by the arts?

- How can you use art to expand your "radar" to see emerging trends?
- Did you gain a better understanding of art by examining the principles used?
- What value is there in art?
- How can you apply what you learned to your own work?
- Do you think work can be a work of art? Why or why not?

Variation

Have the participants explore other art forms such as live theater, popular culture, and the cinema—preferably in a large city.

Contributor

Linda Naiman, BFA, works with organizations to awaken genius-level thinking through the art and science of applying creativity, innovation, and visionary thinking to business strategy. Naiman is a life-long artist and presents workshops on creativity and innovation in North America and Europe.

How to Look at Art
Art educator Edmund B. Feldman developed four stages of looking at art:

1. Identification and Description
Describe what you see. What is the image/sculpture about? Describe the basic elements of the work in terms of colors, lines, and shapes.

2. Analysis
Build on your description by analyzing the work in terms of elements and art principles (for example, aesthetics and composition). Refer to the Arts Principles handout for assistance.

3. Interpretation
What meaning does this work have for you? What is your emotional response to the piece? Share your interpretations with each other and the connections to this piece with aspects of your own lives.

4. Judgment
In your opinion, is this work successful? Why or why not? What relevance does this piece have for you? Revisit the questions related to "what is art for" and discuss what relevance this piece might have to society or the corporate world. What criteria did you use to judge your piece? How has your perception of this artwork changed since you first saw it?

Reproduced from *Orchestrating Collaboration at Work* by Arthur B. VanGundy & Linda Naiman with permission of the publisher. Copyright © 2005 by Arthur B. VanGundy & Linda Naiman.

Arts Principles

Elements of art include the following:

- *Color*—Color is the particular hue that is seen when light is reflected off an object.

- *Form*—Form is flat or three-dimensional (e.g., square, triangle, circle; also cube, pyramid, and sphere).

- *Line*—A line is the visual path created by a moving point.

- *Shape*—The external surface or outline of an object or body.

- *Space*—Space is the area around, within, or between images or elements. Space can be created on a two-dimensional surface by using such techniques as overlapping of objects, varying of object size or placement, varying of color intensity and value, and use of detail and diagonal lines.

- *Figure/Ground*—The relationship between foreground and background or subject and object.

- *Texture*—Texture is the feel or appearance of an object or material.

- *Value*—The lightness or darkness of a color (to create contrast and/or depth). Warm tones advance; cool tones recede.

Principles of art include the following:

- *Aesthetics*—Pertains to sensory perception; a branch of philosophy that provides a theory of beauty and the fine arts. Note that art doesn't have to be beautiful or realistic to be a work of art. Some works of art are meant to shock us, disturb us, or to cause us to question our belief systems or society.

- *Balance*—A feeling of balance results when the elements of design are arranged to create the impression of equality in weight or importance. According to Tim McCreight, "Most of us need balance in the large issues of our lives, things like landscape, architecture, diet, and relationships. Perhaps we look to art and design in the same way we enjoy a roller coaster ride—an opportunity to temporarily suspend our sense of balance in a controlled situation. We know the ride will end, and we know we can turn away from the painting if the lack of stability becomes threatening" (*Design Language*, McCreight, 1997).

- *Composition*—Use of arts principles in arranging or combining elements to form a whole.

- *Contrast*—The placement of opposite elements—color, texture, and so forth—next to one another to create an effect. For example, contrasting colors include red and green. McCreight has written: "Contrast clarifies and heightens an effect. To make a white paper brighter, place a black mark upon it. Punctuate the silence with a scream, the night with a candle, and muted tones with a spot of intense color. Contrast is used to draw attention to an area, to provide stability or clarity in a composition, and to affect the figure/ground relationship, either by clarifying or confusing it."

- *Dialogue*—It has been said that art is a visual dialogue between the viewer and the work of art. Art is a response to a call and art invites a response from the viewer. Dialogue also refers to the interaction between elements—texture, hue, value, or shape—and the association or relationship between the parts.

- *Emphasis*—The special attention or importance given to one part or element in an artwork. Emphasis can be achieved through placement, contrast, size, and so on.

- *Movement*—The way in which the elements of design are organized so that the viewer's eye is led through the work of art in a systematic way.

- *Proportion*—The relationship between objects relative to size, number, and so forth.

- *Repetition*—The repeated use of an element, such as color, shape, or even an object, to create a sense of consistency and continuity in a work of art.

- *Rhythm*—Repetition of elements to create the illusion of movement.

- *Symbolism*—A sign, icon, or image that represents something else by association, resemblance, or convention.

- *Unity*—The coherence of a work that gives the viewer the feeling that all the parts of the piece are working together. As Kenneth Bates has said, "The task of artists is to organize elements into a comprehensible whole by simplifying, organizing and unifying" (From *Design Language* by Tim McCreight. Portland, MA: Byrnmorgen Press. 1997).

EXPRESS YOURSELF

Objectives

- To stimulate visual thinking and multi-sensory processing
- To explore image-making through movement and spontaneity

Uses

- Warm-up
- Communication
- Climate setting

Art Forms

- Painting
- Drawing

Time Required

30 to 45 minutes

Materials, Handouts, and Equipment

- Black calligraphy ink (approximately two tablespoons in a small cup or other container for each participant)
- One calligraphy or watercolor brush (medium) for each participant
- Ten sheets of 11" x 17" bond paper per person
- One jar of water for every two people
- One vase with two to three flowers with uncomplicated shapes such as lilies, birds of paradise, or tulips (another option would be a potted plant with well-defined leaves)

Procedure

1. Divide the participants into small groups of four to seven people.
2. Explain that there is a tradition in the arts (for example, singing, painting, or dance) to warm up and prepare body, mind, and spirit for art-making—to be comfortable with artistic expression—before collaborating in a creative endeavor.

3. Say that you will take them through a series of warm-ups that follow the tradition of Zen calligraphic masters and the teachings of Johannes Itten at the Bauhaus (one of the great art and design schools of the 20th Century). Tell them that Itten said the following:

"If a genuine feeling is to be expressed in a line or plane, this feeling first must resound within the artist. Arm, hand, finger, the whole body, should be permeated with this feeling. Such devotion to work requires concentration and relaxation." (*Design and Form: The Basic Course at the Bauhaus.* New York: Reinhold, 1963)

4. Guide the group through the four relaxation techniques used by Itten to prepare students for an art experience:

    - Tell the group members to sit still and close their eyes. Guide them in focusing on every muscle from their toes to the tops of their heads—first by tightening each muscle, then relaxing it.

    - Ask the group to practice toning by humming and noticing where the tones vibrate in their bodies. Do this for 1 or 2 minutes. Say that Itten asserted, "A tone filled with the powers of the heart can accomplish wonders."

    - Have the group take slow deep breaths for about 1 minute and ask them to "center" themselves while doing so. (Centering can be defined as bringing oneself into balance.)

    - Instruct everyone to apply ink to the tips of their brushes and hold them lightly as they draw a line on paper. Have them practice creating expressive lines, curves, and circles with brush strokes. Tell them to experiment with modifying the pressure of their strokes to achieve variations in their lines.

5. Tell the participants to use their imaginations and draw lines with their brushes that express tightness, speed, tension, flow, and flexibility. Ask them to do this with feeling while imagining that "heart and hand are one." Have them stand up and use their entire arm rather than their hand and wrist to draw.

6. Instruct them to use brush strokes to express the essence of a fish, a rooster, a lion, and flying birds. The objective is to be expressive, quick, and spontaneous. Tell them not to worry about being realistic.

7. Ask everyone to observe the flowers or plant, noting their forms (for example, edges and contours). Instruct them to keep their eyes on the subject and paint its contour and attend to every nuance of the line. Tell them not to look at their art while painting, but to keep their eyes on the subject they are painting.

8. Have them paint the subject again, but this time tell them they may look.

9. Have them compare their two drawings and note any differences.

10. Invite everyone to look at each other's paintings and share their experiences.

Discussion

Use the following questions to facilitate a discussion about the session:

- What thoughts and feelings came up for you in this activity?
- What is your current comfort level with painting?
- What was your comfort level before you began?
- What have you learned from this activity that you can apply to the workplace?

Contributor

Linda Naiman, BFA, works with organizations to awaken genius-level thinking through the art and science of applying creativity, innovation, and visionary thinking to business strategy. Naiman is a life-long artist and presents workshops on creativity and innovation in North America and Europe.

IF YOUR FACE WERE A POEM

Objectives

- To get people's creative juices flowing
- To develop symbolic and metaphorical thinking

Uses

- Warm-up
- Creative thinking
- Getting acquainted

Art Form

Painting

Time Required

30 minutes

Materials, Handouts, and Equipment

For each participant:

- At least five different colors of tempura paint or colored markers
- Two sheets of bond paper
- One ½" or ¾" paint brush (if using paint)
- One small container of water (if using paint)

Procedure

1. Organize the participants into small groups of four to seven people sitting at small tables.

2. Say aloud, "If your face were a poem, what would it look like? Think of symbols and metaphors using color, shape, and texture to make a self-portrait. Add words or verse if you wish. Be open to 'happy accidents.'"

3. Tell them to start drawing or painting their pictures.

4. After everyone has finished, have them share their pictures with each other and ask for positive feedback from the other group members.

Discussion

Conduct a discussion using the following questions:

- What does your picture tell the world about you?
- What insights do the pictures provide you about other group members?
- What have you learned about yourself and each other in this process?
- To what extent do you think others projected their ideal selves into the pictures?

Variation

Provide each participant with mask-making materials (markers, cellophane tape, glitter, glue, yarn, and so forth), scissors, and cardboard. Have participants create a mask based on the same question: If your face were a poem, what would it look like?

Contributor

Linda Naiman, BFA, works with organizations to awaken genius-level thinking through the art and science of applying creativity, innovation, and visionary thinking to business strategy. Naiman is a life-long artist and presents workshops on creativity and innovation in North America and Europe.

RESTRICTIONS AND LIMITATIONS

Objectives

- To provide an introduction to "art-making"
- To create a foundation to enhance the arts experience in more complex activities
- To overcome fear of art
- To get creative juices flowing
- To experiment with color

Uses

- Arts warm-up
- Creative thinking
- Innovation

Art Form

Painting

Time Required

15 minutes

Materials, Handouts, and Equipment

- One tube of each color paint for each participant: blue-cyan, red-magenta, yellow, and black
- Three sheets of paper for each participant
- One brush for each participant
- Containers for paint and water for each participant
- One roll of paper towels for every five participants
- Any full-color picture with printer's proof marks (showing the squares along the edge of the page in CMYK—cyan, magenta, yellow, and black). Ask your neighborhood printer for a sample. One picture per participant.

Procedure

1. Instruct the participants as follows:

   - Dab the three primary colors (red, blue, and yellow) in their pure form onto your paper.

   - Create as many color combinations as you can from the three primary colors and add these to your page.

   - For the sake of order, make a grid out of your dabs of color. For instance, you might have three rows of three dabs each to create a nine-dot grid. Do this quickly—you are making visual notes, not a work of art.

   - Add black and continue making new colors.

2. Call time and show the printer's proof and explain that all the colors of the picture came from three primary colors plus black.

Discussion

The following questions can be used to help guide a discussion:

- Variations of these three colors form the full spectrum of the rainbow. How many different colors did you create?

- What parallel exists between this exercise and the composition of teams?

- This exercise demonstrates the unlimited possibilities derived from limitations and restrictions. What restrictions and limitations does your team have to deal with?

- How might you use the creativity of your work team to overcome such limitations?

Contributor

Linda Naiman, BFA, works with organizations to awaken genius-level thinking through the art and science of applying creativity, innovation, and visionary thinking to business strategy. Naiman is a life-long artist and presents workshops on creativity and innovation in North America and Europe.

STRIKE UP THE BAND

Objectives

- To improve listening skills
- To improve presentation skills
- To improve decision-making skills
- To improve the ability to think abstractly

Uses

- Arts warm-up
- Team building
- Communication

Art Forms

- Music
- Improvisation

Time Required

20 to 30 minutes

Materials, Handouts, and Equipment

- One kazoo for each participant
- Rubbing alcohol and cotton balls in resealable plastic bags (to sterilize the kazoos for subsequent groups or allow current participants to sterilize again)

Procedure

1. Distribute the kazoos to all participants.
2. Allow participants to sterilize their kazoos, if desired.
3. Demonstrate how to play the kazoo. Tell participants that kazoos require a sound like singing or humming to go through the instrument, not just air. Hum on your kazoo to demonstrate.

4. Reassure them that they are allowed to sound "goofy." That's the whole idea. They shouldn't worry about what others think of their playing skills.

5. Give them at least 1 minute to practice playing their kazoos and become comfortable with them.

6. Explain that you first will play a musical sentence called a "phrase," and they then should copy you. Do this a couple of times so they can get the hang of it. Use phrases from Christmas songs, nursery rhymes, popular songs, rock, classical, or any tunes known to the group.

7. Next, try phrases of unfamiliar tunes in fragments so that they cannot anticipate what is next, but must rely on their listening skills. (Keep these tune fragments short so the group can remember them and reproduce what you played.)

8. Ask for participants to volunteer and play a brief sample of what they just did.

9. Explain that you will create a phrase in the form of a question. Invite individuals and then groups of people to answer you with an original musical thought in response.

Discussion

Lead a discussion using the following questions:

- How uncomfortable were you with the exercise at the start? At the end?
- Can you see similarities and differences between this exercise and how comfortable your team is in brainstorming new ideas?
- How might you use these similarities and differences to improve team performance?
- What general implications are there for group collaboration?

Variation

Ask musical questions using music phrases by humming to individuals in a circle so all can respond individually and they have the choice to answer or not. If they don't want to respond, they can say, "pass," and the next person can decide whether or not to respond. This can be scary for some people, so don't push them. Let it flow and don't judge those who don't wish to participate.

Your last call and response can be some familiar song with a known response such as humming through the Kazoo, "shave and a haircut." The participants then would respond by humming, "two bits" on their kazoos.

Contributor

Janice Kilgore has varied experiences in the professional music world as well as being a devout music educator and musician. She was trained at the University of North Texas with degrees in music education (B.M., M.M.E.). She is currently working on a doctorate at UNT in creative thinking through music education applications. She has served as a consultant and lecturer since 1987 and is in over ten editions of *Who's Who*, including *Who's Who in Entertainment*. Ms. Kilgore has created a distance learning music education program for children and contributed to several exercises in *101 Great Games and Activities* (Pfeiffer). She is currently on staff at Tarrant County College, Southeast Campus, as a music instructor.

THINKING SYMBOLICALLY

Objectives

- To create a foundation to enhance an arts experience in more complex activities
- To overcome fear of art
- To enhance creative thinking

Uses

- Nonverbal communication
- Creative thinking
- Climate setting
- Getting acquainted

Art Forms

- Painting
- Drawing
- Abstraction

Time Required

20 minutes

Materials, Handouts, and Equipment

For each participant:

- Tempera paints, watercolor, or colored markers
- Paper (approximately 18" x 24")
- A brush, ½" to 1")
- A container for water
- A copy of the Universal Symbols handout

Procedure

1. Explain that you will guide people in a visualization exercise of self-awareness through symbolism.

2. Have them sit in a comfortable position, get quiet, relax, close their eyes, and breathe deeply. Say:

   "Gather your thoughts and let go of any 'mind chatter,' any worries that take you out of the present moment. With each breath you take, you are more relaxed, your emotions are calm, and your mind is still. From this place of calm and quiet, sink deep into the essence of your being. Search for the part of you that is wise and all-knowing, for the symbol that best expresses who you really are. Try to think of the symbol that best expresses your true nature. In a state of relaxation, stay in the silence and wait for a symbol to come to you."

3. Tell them to begin painting or drawing their symbols when ready. These symbols might be geometric or animal images. They also might be feelings. If so, give them a form.

4. When everyone has finished, ask everyone to share their experiences in finding a symbol and explain its meaning as well.

5. Distribute a copy of the Universal Symbols handout to each participant. Give them a few minutes to review it and then lead a discussion.

Discussion

Lead a discussion using the following questions:

- How does your symbol compare to the universal symbols in your handout?
- If you have a goal to achieve, it may help to create a symbol to help make it real. What aspects of your work, team, or organization can you look at symbolically?
- How might symbolism help improve team communications?
- What are some of the obstacles to symbolic communication?

Variation

Rather than first trying to come up with a symbol, start by asking everyone to think, "Who am I?" and writing down the first three words that come to mind. Then create a symbol that synthesizes these words.

Contributor

Linda Naiman, BFA, works with organizations to awaken genius-level thinking through the art and science of applying creativity, innovation, and visionary thinking to business strategy. Naiman is a life-long artist and presents workshops on creativity and innovation in North America and Europe.

Universal Symbols

The painter Paul Cezanne said, "Everything in nature takes its form from the sphere, the cone, and the cylinder." These form the six universal shapes/symbols. Some of their messages are described below. What meanings do these symbols have for you?

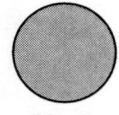

Circle
Wholeness
Unity
The self
Eternity
The heavens
Cyclic

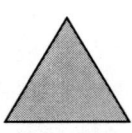

Triangle
Trinity
Unity in diversity
Three-fold nature of universe—
body, soul, and spirit

Square
Stability
Earth
Static perfection
Permanence
Mystical union of
four elements
Order

Spiral
Growth
Change
Continuity
Generativity
Creativity

Star
Divinity
Highest attainment
Hope
Creation/union of masculine
and feminine principles
Seal of Solomon

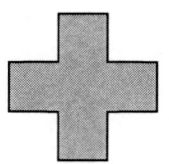

Cross
Integration
Universal archetypal man
Descent of spirit
into matter
Eternal life
Union of opposites

Reproduced from *Orchestrating Collaboration at Work* by Arthur B. VanGundy & Linda Naiman with permission of the publisher. Copyright © 2005 by Arthur B. VanGundy & Linda Naiman.

TRANSPARENCY

Objectives

- To create a foundation to enhance arts experiences
- To get your creative juices flowing

Uses

- Warm-up
- Nonverbal communication
- Creative thinking
- Climate setting

Art Forms

- Collage
- Design

Time Required

40 minutes

Materials, Handouts, and Equipment

- Colored tissue paper
- White construction paper
- White glue

Procedure

1. Have individuals in small groups of four to seven people begin by creating an image from a preconceived idea about team collaboration.

2. Tell them to experiment with colors and shape by intuitively ripping tissue paper and arranging it in a pleasing manner.

3. Tell them to glue their shapes onto a piece of construction paper. If the colors and shapes start to suggest an emerging theme, they should elaborate. The idea here is to be open and spontaneous. (An advantage of tissue paper is its transparency and capacity to reveal surprising new colors and form.)

Discussion

Lead a discussion using the following questions:

- To what extent did the element of transparency contribute to your art experience?
- What was the difference in your experience between the first and second picture?
- To what extent did you try to control the outcome of your picture?
- What did you most enjoy about working with this medium?
- Compare the value of transparency in art to the value of transparency in leadership in teams and organizations. How might transparency be a useful metaphor relative to innovation?
- To what extent is team collaboration in general "transparent"?
- To what extent should your team become more transparent in its collaborative activities? How might you make this happen?

Contributor

Linda Naiman, BFA, works with organizations to awaken genius-level thinking through the art and science of applying creativity, innovation, and visionary thinking to business strategy. Naiman is a life-long artist and presents workshops on creativity and innovation in North America and Europe.

5 Collage/Mixed Media

- Candid Collages
- The Figure/Ground of Conflict
- Golden Moment
- Just Suppose Juxtapose
- Mapping Your Future
- People Wall
- Searching for Genius in All the Unexpected Places
- Self-Portrait
- Shift Happens

CANDID COLLAGES

Objectives

- To vividly identify and share employees' negative and positive perceptions about corporate change
- To stimulate recognition of the need for change within a team or organization
- To build support for change
- To suggest ways to promote a smoother transition

Uses

- Preparation for instituting structural or cultural change within organizations (for example, management reorganizations, mergers, company name changes)
- Change management that deals specifically with attitudes, values, and motivation
- Soliciting authentic viewpoints of participants

Art Form

Collage

Time Required

Approximately 90 minutes to 2 hours

Materials, Handouts, and Equipment

- One large foam core board (or mat board), approximately 20" x 30," for each team
- Assortment of magazines that cover a range of subjects (travel, entertainment, technology, business, fashion, cooking, photography), at least five magazines per group
- Scissors, at least two pairs for every three people
- Scotch® tape and/or glue stick, at least two for every three people

Procedure

1. Divide participants into equal-sized teams of three to six people.
2. Give each team one set of materials.
3. Ask half the teams to create collages from magazine images that depict the current, pre-change team or company environment (that is, "Who are we today?").
4. Ask the other teams to each create a collage from magazine images that depicts how they perceive the post-change team or company environment or ideal situation (that is, "What will the company be like after the change?" or "Who are we capable of being?").
5. Tell the participants that they have free reign to rip and cut the magazines. They also may trade them among the teams.
6. Inform the participants that they will have 20 minutes to leaf through the magazines to find relevant images. They will have an additional 20 minutes to compose their collages. Give the participants periodic time updates.
7. Ask each team to present its collage to the entire group (that is, describe why each image was chosen, what each image connotes, how the images were ordered, and the significance of the proximity of images to each other).

Discussion

After all teams have presented their collages, lead a discussion comparing and contrasting similarities and differences of the pre-change environment to that of the post-change environment. Continue with questions such as:

- How might the team or company benefit, internally and externally, by capitalizing on its strengths and positive attributes, pre- and post-change?
- How might the team or company smoothly move from the current situation to the future one with the least amount of interruption and dissonance for employees?
- What ideas do you have to help overcome the perceived obstacles (or myths) associated with the future post-change environment?

Contributor

Holly M. O'Neill is founder and principal of Talking Business, a marketing consultancy specializing in strategy, branding, marketing research, and product planning. By integrating creativity with structure, Talking Business delivers breakthrough concepts and solutions, which optimize clients' marketing efforts and accelerate their visionary initiatives.

THE FIGURE/GROUND OF CONFLICT

Objectives

- To work through negative judgments that create blocks for groups
- To help people see how they create and can alter their experiences

Uses

- Team building
- Managing change

Art Form

Collage

Time Required

Approximately 2 hours

Materials, Handouts, and Equipment

- A copy of the Figure/Ground handout for each participant
- Children's poster paints or water colors for everyone
- ¼" to ¾" bristle brushes for all participants
- 11" x 17" bond paper for each participant
- Construction paper in assorted colors for each participant
- Scissors for every two participants
- A large pile of magazines for images
- White glue or rubber cement
- Paper towels
- Ice cube trays or other small containers for paint for each participant
- Individual containers for water

Procedure

1. Form participants into small groups of four to seven people each (actual work teams if possible).

2. Have each subgroup think of five to ten negative judgments or perceptions that block their work team's success. Encourage them to achieve consensus and pick one.

3. Distribute the Figure/Ground handout and instruct the participants to read it.

4. Provide each person a large piece of paper and tell them to paint a "background" that represents the psychological climate of their work unit.

5. Ask them to think about the event, decision, or action that led to this "negative" experience and list their interpretations, assumptions, and judgments related to it.

6. Invite them to cut out shapes or pictures from magazines that represent their interpretations, assumptions, and judgments and place them on the background in a way that represents their current experience (this is known as a "collage").

7. Discuss different people's collages. Ask them to describe their backgrounds—their perceptions of the current climate—and note the differences among their perceptions.

Discussion

Lead a discussion using the following questions:

- How are the judgments people made about the event colored by the background of the climate they perceive in the organization?

- Notice the variety of experiences the exercise has generated. Who is having the "right" experience? (The "correct" answer is "everyone.") Emphasize that each of us creates our own experiences and they emerge from the background of the assumptions and interpretations we have about our teams and the organization. Yet many of these assumptions and interpretations rest on very little factual information.

- What other interpretations and judgments might people have about this exercise and events in general in their teams? What might they like to have?

- What kind of background assumptions about others and the team or organizational climate would people need to have those interpretations and judgments?

- What do you need to do to get a more grounded story about the background of your team and organization based on solid information? How might you obtain this information?

Variation

Have participants paint a positive team or organizational climate (background) and compare differences after using the above procedure. Place the same figure collage on that background and discuss how the experience changes.

Contributors

Gervase Bushe, Ph.D., is an associate professor at Simon Fraser University in Vancouver, B.C., Canada. He has over twenty-five years of experience consulting in executive leadership, planned change, team building, and organizational redesign. His award-winning articles appear in numerous publications. His most recent book is *Clear Leadership*.

Linda Naiman, BFA, works with organizations to awaken genius-level thinking through the art and science of applying creativity, innovation, and visionary thinking to business strategy. Naiman is a life-long artist and presents workshops on creativity and innovation in North America and Europe.

Figure/Ground

Figure/ground in art refers to the relationship between the foreground and the background—or the relationship between the subject and the object. The figure/ground relationship is defined by the structure/design/organization of shapes that make up the composition of a picture.

The three-dimensional equivalent of the figure/ground relationship is the positive/negative dynamic of form and space. When drawing objects, it's helpful to look at the negative space (the space surrounding a chair for example) as a way to define the positive space—the chair itself.

The degree of tension or harmony between the subject and object is accomplished by contrast in elements such as color, shape, position, and size. The greatest contrast in color is black and yellow (which is why road signs in North America use those colors).

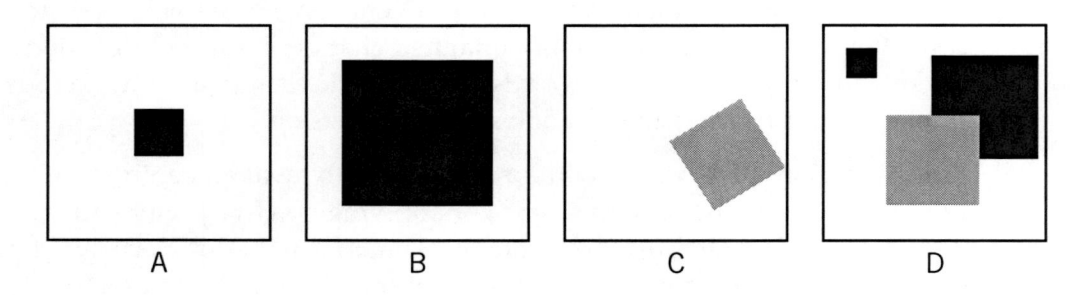

A   B   C   D

Examine the elements of shape, size, position, and "color" of subject and object in these layouts. A small figure in the middle of an immense background imparts a different visual/emotional impact than a large figure with almost no background. For example, there is more visual tension in C than A because of its proximity to the edge of the box. Figure/ground is also established by overlapping objects as in D. The painter Hans Hoffmann and other abstract expressionists tried to make the figure/ground dynamic ambiguous through the interplay of subject and object so that neither dominated. This is illustrated best by the Tao (below), a symbol of the unity and harmony of yin and yang—the guiding principle of all reality.

Reproduced from *Orchestrating Collaboration at Work* by Arthur B. VanGundy & Linda Naiman with permission of the publisher. Copyright © 2003 by John Wiley & Sons, Inc.

GOLDEN MOMENT

Objectives

- To identify the energizing, life-giving forces in a group or organization
- To build rapport and a positive environment in a group
- To build a common vision of a great work environment

Uses

- Team building
- Visioning

Art Form

Collage

Time Required

60 to 90 minutes

Materials, Handouts, and Equipment

Enough of the following materials for each participant to construct a collage:

- Children's poster paints or water colors
- Bristle brushes (¼" to ¾")
- Bond paper (11" x 17")
- Construction paper in assorted colors
- Scissors
- A large pile of magazines for images
- White glue or rubber cement
- Paper towels
- Ice cube trays or other small containers for paint
- Containers for water

Procedure

1. Divide participants into small groups of four to seven people.
2. Ask the participants to think about the "golden moments" in their work lives—times when they felt most alive, energized, and inspired.
3. Have them individually make a collage or painting that depicts such a time in their work lives.
4. Tell them to describe the collage or painting and its meaning to others in their small groups. Have others respond to their descriptions.
5. Suggest that they use these meanings to brainstorm ways to improve team collaboration.

Discussion

Lead a discussion with the whole group using the following questions:

- What common themes emerged from your collages?
- What brings energy and vitality to your art?
- What are the things that bring energy and vitality to your team and organizations?
- Is there a connection between the two?
- How can you ensure there is an abundant supply in your team and organization?

Contributors

Gervase Bushe, Ph.D., is an associate professor at Simon Fraser University in Vancouver, B.C., Canada. He has over twenty-five years of experience consulting in executive leadership, planned change, team building, and organizational redesign. His award-winning articles appear in numerous publications. His most recent book is *Clear Leadership*.

Linda Naiman, BFA, works with organizations to awaken genius-level thinking through the art and science of applying creativity, innovation, and visionary thinking to business strategy. Naiman is a life-long artist and presents workshops on creativity and innovation in North America and Europe.

JUST SUPPOSE JUXTAPOSE

Objectives

- To improve creative collaboration skills in teams
- To enhance idea-generation skills

Uses

- Creative thinking
- Problem solving
- Collaboration
- Team building

Art Form

Mixed media collage

Time Required

60 minutes

Materials, Handouts, and Equipment

- Enough of the following materials for each individual to create a collage:
  - Assorted media: interesting headlines and advertising from magazines or newspapers
  - Lists of best-selling of books, music, and movies (obtain from Internet websites)
  - Paper (poster-sized)
  - Glue
  - Scissors
  - Colored markers
- Writing paper for each participant
- A pen or pencil for each participant

Procedure

1. Explain the meaning of "juxtaposition" to the participants: placing unrelated elements side by side to produce unexpected combinations of colors, shapes, and ideas. Artists and poets use juxtaposition to create new meanings out of unexpected relationships from images or words.

2. Distribute paper and a pen or pencil to each participant.

3. Instruct the participants to think of a project they are working on and identify some problems they are experiencing. Have them choose one compelling challenge.

4. Tell them to break down this problem into smaller components (Who? What? Where? When? Why? How?) and write down at least one statement for each aspect of the problem. For instance, consider the problem: "How might we increase employee retention?" A smaller part of this problem might be: "When do we want to retain employees?" One answer would be: "During peak production periods." This answer might be used to redefine the problem as, "How might we increase production?"

5. Divide the participants into groups of four and distribute the collage-making materials.

6. Ask each group to work on one or two problem statements. Instruct them to sift through the ads, headlines, lists, et cetera and juxtapose them with the problem statements. For instance, select an ad and combine it with an element of the problem to suggest an idea. For the retention problem, an idea might arise from juxtaposing it with an ad for a new car. In this case, the idea might be to provide free transportation to employees at risk of leaving.

7. Tell groups to make a collage based on their juxtapositions and the ideas they have generated. Include problem solutions in the collages, written out.

8. Have all groups reconvene to show their work and tell their stories.

Discussion

Use the following questions to help guide a discussion:

- What new connections can you make from "juxtapositioning"?
- What hidden patterns emerged?
- What insights have you discovered?

- What can you apply to your work? Your team?
- Look at the collection of images and headlines you have chosen. What does this say about the group's mood, culture, et cetera?
- What clues might this collection provide you about the future?

Contributors

Linda Naiman, BFA, works with organizations to awaken genius-level thinking through the art and science of applying creativity, innovation, and visionary thinking to business strategy. Naiman is a life-long artist and presents workshops on creativity and innovation in North America and Europe.

Arthur VanGundy, president of VanGundy & Associates, works as a creativity consultant, trainer, and facilitator of brainstorming retreats. He is the author of ten books, including *Techniques of Structured Problem Solving, Training Your Creative Mind, Managing Group Creativity, Brain Boosters for Business Advantage,* and *101 Great Games & Activities.* Major clients include Hershey Foods, S.C. Johnson Company, Xerox, Motorola, Sunbeam, Air Canada, Monsanto, Wyeth-Ayerst Pharmaceuticals, and the Singapore government. He also is founder of All Star Minds, a global Internet brainstorming service.

MAPPING YOUR FUTURE

Objectives

- To use visuals to clarify challenges
- To organize information into a story or plan
- To develop a shared vision of the future

Uses

- Leadership
- Values
- Nonverbal communication
- Creative thinking
- Group identity
- Community building
- Organization development

Art Forms

- Collage
- Storytelling

Time Required

2 hours

Materials, Handouts, and Equipment

- Enough of the following for each group to create a collage:
  - Pencils
  - Markers
  - Paper (18" x 24")
  - Non-permanent adhesive
  - Scissors or X-ACTO® knives
  - Pictures of different scenes in the participants' organization
  - A stack of picture-filled magazines

- In addition, for each group:
  - Flipchart paper and stand
  - Post-it® Notes
  - Roll of butcher paper
  - Flipchart paper, stand, and markers

Procedure*

1. Ask the participants to form into subgroups of four.

2. Provide each group with collage-making materials. Tell the groups they will be constructing maps of the future for the team. Have them include a timeline showing where they have come from to where they are now to where they would like to be in the future.

3. To mark events, have them use images from magazines, words, and drawings to tell their stories. Just as maps have legends to choose the best routes, they should consider possible routes to their destinations and what that means in terms of resources required. Say:

   "Be creative and expressive. Think of the best shapes for your maps. Linear? Funnel-shaped? Is it a train track with multiple offshoots? Use your maps/collages to tell your stories and generate enthusiasm."

4. Have each subgroup show its map to the whole group and tell its story. Invite questions from the audience.

5. Ask for a volunteer to record on the flipchart the similarities and differences in the stories.

6. Tell each subgroup to decide what the most important elements of its map are.

7. Tell the participants that they will now make a new map on a roll of paper to capture key concepts.

8. Instruct participants to extract pictures from the original maps to add to the new map. Tell them they can add words and pictures to illustrate desired outcomes in one year and then five years.

---

* Note: This activity is designed to be conducted with participants from the same organization.

9. Invite participants to make remarks on Post-it® Notes and add them to the map.

10. Ask participants to discuss implications of the new map (as a shared vision) for individual teams or the organization in general. Decide what actions need to be taken.

Discussion

Use the following questions to lead a discussion:

- What have you learned from the stories?
- What might apply to team collaboration?
- How similar or different is your idea of the future from those of others?
- Do you believe you can make your "map to the future" a reality?
- To make this real, what changes need to be made? What actions must be taken?

Contributor

Linda Naiman, BFA, works with organizations to awaken genius-level thinking through the art and science of applying creativity, innovation, and visionary thinking to business strategy. Naiman is a life-long artist and presents workshops on creativity and innovation in North America and Europe.

PEOPLE WALL

Objectives

- To create a mural that tells the story of a team or organization
- To develop visual thinking skills
- To improve creative collaboration skills
- To improve visual workspaces

Uses

- Nonverbal communication
- Creative thinking
- Group identity
- Community building
- Corporate culture
- Collaboration

Art Forms

- Painting
- Collage

Time Required

3 hours

Materials, Handouts, and Equipment

- Enough of the following for each group to create a collage:
    - Acrylic or poster paints
    - Poster-size paper or foam board (For something more permanent, use wood panels, grouped so they form a mural. If working with plywood, cover it with gesso first—available at art supply stores.)
    - Large paint brushes
    - Containers for paint (if needed) and water
    - Paper towels

- Scissors
- Glue
- Objects or pictures relevant to the team or organization culture
- Digital camera
- Color printer
- Computer or other device to view web images

Procedure

1. Assign the participants to small groups of four to seven people or into natural work units.

2. Ask the participants to review the pictures and use them to help recall stories team members have told about who they are, what they stand for, and where they are going as a team.

3. Ask them about what ideas they get from this review relative to creating a "People Wall" (that is, a mural depicting themes, team spirit, culture, and energy expressed by the people).

4. Show participants the work of Jim Dine and Robert Rauschenberg for inspiration. You can find examples of their images at www.thinker.org/fam/index_thinker.asp. Go to the bottom of the page and enter either "Dine" or "Rauschenberg" in "The Thinker" image base "keywords" box.

5. Have the participants take photographs of each other (and others if appropriate). Print them out as large as possible.

6. Instruct them to work together to develop a collage of images and objects on paper, foam, or plywood panels. When they have created a satisfactory arrangement, have the participants glue their collages to the panels.

7. Tell them to use painting as a means of linking different images to create cohesion. They may paint over the edges of cut-out pictures to help blend them together. They should feel free to include words or phrases and people's names.

8. Instruct them to mount their final collages on a wall and discuss with team members or participants from other groups.

Discussion

Use the following questions to help guide a discussion:

- What did you experience during this collaborative exercise?
- What feelings were evoked during this process?
- Was this a satisfying experience? Why or why not?
- Are you pleased with the results? If not what would you change?
- What did you learn from this activity that you could apply to your work? To your team?

Contributor

Linda Naiman, BFA, works with organizations to awaken genius-level thinking through the art and science of applying creativity, innovation, and visionary thinking to business strategy. Naiman is a life-long artist and presents workshops on creativity and innovation in North America and Europe.

SEARCHING FOR GENIUS IN ALL THE UNEXPECTED PLACES

Objectives

- To foster collaborative learning and problem solving
- To provide an adventure in innovation thinking
- To apply breakthrough insights and ideas in ways that can turn business enterprises around, grow them dramatically, or simply make them more efficient, effective, and successful

Uses

- Energizer
- Team building
- Business development

Art Forms

- Drawing
- Photography
- Storytelling

Time Required

1 to 3 hours

Materials, Handouts, and Equipment

- Paper and pencil for each group
- One Polaroid® camera (with film) for each group to document what they discover on their treasure hunt
- A copy of the Questions as Catalysts for Discovery and Discussion handout for each participant
- "Arts and crafts" materials such as blocks of foam, glitter, ribbon, flowers, yarn, paints, markers, et cetera (make available for presentations, if participants want to use them)

Procedure

1. Divide participants into small groups of two or three "discoverers."

2. Have them select a challenge in their work or a way to improve a business strategy and action.

3. Provide each group with a Polaroid® camera, paper, and pencil. Tell the groups they will be embarking on an outdoor expedition to find examples of nature's original creations (for example, the branching structures of trees, plant life, the fractal-like forms of water, weather patterns, rock formations, and so forth).

4. Tell them to search anywhere around their immediate environments to look for examples of exceptional ingenuity exhibited by nature. They should try to identify at least five examples, take a photo of each, and document any insights and discoveries in writing.

5. Ask participants to return within an appropriate time frame (½ hour to 2 hours, depending on amount of total time available).

6. Once everyone has returned, tell participants to use their "genius strokes" (creativity) to catalyze their thinking on the specific business issues they identified earlier. They should identify many possible new solutions based on a connection to one of their examples of nature's ingenuity. Encourage them to explore bold ways of using their examples to stimulate further breakthrough thinking.

7. Distribute a copy of the Questions as Catalysts for Discovery and Discussion handout to each participant to spark additional ideas.

8. Instruct each group to decide whether or not any of its possible new solutions represent a quantum leap for a specific project.

9. Have the groups use any medium preferred to develop a 5-minute presentation. This documentation can be expressed in simple visual or written notations. The presentation should address the following:

    - Why the idea is an innovation (that is, a modification of an original invention)

    - How this stroke of genius can be connected to one of their current projects to make a significant difference

    - Whether this new innovation is a possible quantum leap or just a good idea

    - Other ways this innovation(s) could be used by the team or organization

Discussion

After each team has had a chance to present, lead a discussion using the following questions:

- What does your business look and feel like today?

- Describe your business environment. Is it simple, orderly, healthy, meaningful, and connected to the rest of the world? Or is it stressful, at the breakneck speed of an increasingly complex, chaotic hyper-civilization that remains conceptually fragmented and socially disconnected?

- Do your business practices embody or live the American Indian word, "Koyaanisqatsi," which means "life out of balance"?

- If nature is the quintessential embodiment of unbounded creativity, learning, and communication, what are some ways you can learn from the natural world to help your company grow and sustain its growth by better customizing and personalizing your company's products and services?

Contributor

Todd Siler, Ph.D., is the founder of Psi-Phi Communications (now Think Like a Genius, LLC), which develops learning materials and tools for accelerating breakthroughs and innovations in businesses, schools, cultural organizations, and families. He is a visual artist, inventor, and author whose publications, *Think Like a Genius* and *Breaking the Mind Barrier,* have been translated into many languages. Over the past decade, Dr. Siler has facilitated Think Like a Genius® workshops with many Fortune 500 companies, including IBM, Chevron, Chase Manhattan, ING North America, Procter & Gamble, and Nabisco, as well as leading Internet companies, such as NTT/Verio, and venture capital businesses, SoftBank (Mobius), and Centennial Ventures.

Questions as Catalysts for Discovery and Discussion

Think about:

- A fire ant's ability to defend itself
- A sprawling root system
- The turbulence of water, wind, and electrical currents
- Discontinuous geological patterns of growth
- Paradoxical environmental forces
- The sharp vision of an eagle
- Dangers of an uncharted wilderness
- The chaotic actions of an angry crowd

Consider these questions:

- What do these elements of nature have in common with the natural elements of business?
- How does the business of life mirror the life of business?
- How can your group follow in the footsteps of some of history's greatest innovators and discoverers, who looked to nature not only to inspire them, but also to provide them with deep insights and clues to innovation? Among them are Leonardo da Vinci, Thomas Edison, Marie Curie, Barbara McClintock, R. Buckminster Fuller, Alexander Fleming, and Pablo Picasso. How have these innovative thinkers used the arts in partnership with the sciences to help us discover our deeper connections with the whole of nature?
- How does nature generously provides us with a world of clues for lifting our minds to new heights of achievement?
- How does our creative freedom reward us with innovations of flight and flights of innovation, which grow new roots in our ever-curious nerve cells?

SELF-PORTRAIT

Objectives

- To explore the self in relation to the team
- To stimulate visual thinking and multi-sensory processing
- To explore abstraction as a means of compressing and synthesizing information
- To construct knowledge and meaning from art

Uses

- Communication
- Climate setting
- Learning organizations
- Getting acquainted

Art Form

Collage

Time Required

Approximately 45 minutes

Materials, Handouts, and Equipment

- At least five sheets of colored construction paper for each person
- One pair of scissors for each person
- One container of glue or a glue stick for each person
- A copy of the Arts Principles handout per person

Procedure

1. Tell participants that this activity involves creating an expressive self-portrait—through distortion and abstraction—by cutting and ripping shapes out of paper.

2. Read this quote:

   "Picasso and DeKooning have sought, through distortion and abstraction, to capture underlying truths of our physical selves." (Robert Shapiro, *Art Journal*, Spring 1996, College Art Association)

3. Distribute a copy of the Arts Principles handout to each participant and give the group a few minutes to review it.

4. Instruct participants to create a portrait using distortion and abstraction to represent how they see themselves in the workplace. Tell them to be spontaneous and, without thinking too much, cut out, tear, or rip paper to create shapes. (Torn paper has a softer edge and can be used to contrast the hard edge of cut paper.) Remind them not to be realistic with their shapes—be expressive and creative. Advise them to move shapes around in a pleasing way, paying attention to form, movement, composition, edges of the page, and color.

5. Have each participant, in turn, share his or her self-portrait with other group members and discuss implications for team identity and performance.

Discussion

Use the following questions to help guide the discussion:

- What effect have you created?
- What does your picture say about you and your work team?
- How difficult was it to create shapes by cutting and tearing?
- How much or how little control did you have?
- How did that affect your creative output?

Contributor

Linda Naiman, BFA, works with organizations to awaken genius-level thinking through the art and science of applying creativity, innovation, and visionary thinking to business strategy. Naiman is a life-long artist and presents workshops on creativity and innovation in North America and Europe.

Arts Principles

Elements of art include the following:

- *Color*—Color is the particular hue that is seen when light is reflected off an object.

- *Form*—Form is flat or three-dimensional (e.g., square, triangle, circle; also cube, pyramid, and sphere).

- *Line*—A line is the visual path created by a moving point.

- *Shape*—The external surface or outline of an object or body.

- *Space*—Space is the area around, within, or between images or elements. Space can be created on a two-dimensional surface by using such techniques as overlapping of objects, varying of object size or placement, varying of color intensity and value, and use of detail and diagonal lines.

- *Figure/Ground*—The relationship between foreground and background or subject and object.

- *Texture*—Texture is the feel or appearance of an object or material.

- *Value*—The lightness or darkness of a color (to create contrast and/or depth). Warm tones advance; cool tones recede.

Principles of art include the following:

- *Aesthetics*—Pertains to sensory perception; a branch of philosophy that provides a theory of beauty and the fine arts. Note that art doesn't have to be beautiful or realistic to be a work of art. Some works of art are meant to shock us, disturb us, or to cause us to question our belief systems or society.

- *Balance*—A feeling of balance results when the elements of design are arranged to create the impression of equality in weight or importance. According to Tim McCreight, "Most of us need balance in the large issues of our lives, things like landscape, architecture, diet, and relationships. Perhaps we look to art and design in the same way we enjoy a roller coaster ride—an opportunity to temporarily suspend our sense of balance in a controlled situation. We know the ride will end, and we know we can turn away from the painting if the lack of stability becomes threatening" (*Design Language*, McCreight, 1997).

Reproduced from *Orchestrating Collaboration at Work* by Arthur B. VanGundy & Linda Naiman with permission of the publisher. Copyright © 2003 by John Wiley & Sons, Inc.

- *Composition*—Use of arts principles in arranging or combining elements to form a whole.

- *Contrast*—The placement of opposite elements—color, texture, and so forth—next to one another to create an effect. For example, contrasting colors include red and green. McCreight has written: "Contrast clarifies and heightens an effect. To make a white paper brighter, place a black mark upon it. Punctuate the silence with a scream, the night with a candle, and muted tones with a spot of intense color. Contrast is used to draw attention to an area, to provide stability or clarity in a composition, and to affect the figure/ground relationship, either by clarifying or confusing it."

- *Dialogue*—It has been said that art is a visual dialogue between the viewer and the work of art. Art is a response to a call and art invites a response from the viewer. Dialogue also refers to the interaction between elements—texture, hue, value, or shape—and the association or relationship between the parts.

- *Emphasis*—The special attention or importance given to one part or element in an artwork. Emphasis can be achieved through placement, contrast, size, and so on.

- *Movement*—The way in which the elements of design are organized so that the viewer's eye is led through the work of art in a systematic way.

- *Proportion*—The relationship between objects relative to size, number, and so forth.

- *Repetition*—The repeated use of an element, such as color, shape, or even an object, to create a sense of consistency and continuity in a work of art.

- *Rhythm*—Repetition of elements to create the illusion of movement.

- *Symbolism*—A sign, icon, or image that represents something else by association, resemblance, or convention.

- *Unity*—The coherence of a work that gives the viewer the feeling that all the parts of the piece are working together. As Kenneth Bates has said, "The task of artists is to organize elements into a comprehensible whole by simplifying, organizing and unifying" (From *Design Language* by Tim McCreight. Portland, MA: Byrnmorgen Press. 1997).

SHIFT HAPPENS

Objectives

- To learn how to adapt to changes
- To experience the emotional and visceral effects of change and its resistance
- To become more receptive to change
- To demonstrate that creative solutions often require destruction of what already exists

Uses

- Team building
- Change management
- Consensus building
- Tapping into creativity
- Collaboration

Art Form

Design

Time Required

45 to 60 minutes

Materials, Handouts, and Equipment

- Tables with chairs for four to ten people per table
- One flipchart or overhead projector with blank transparencies for each group
- One CD player and instrumental music appropriate to the mood you want to create (for example, soothing, active). (Please observe all copyright laws regarding playing music.)
- Five sheets of 8.5" x 11" colored paper for each participant
- One glue stick for every three people
- One pair of scissors for every three people

- Colored markers for each person
- Art supplies for each group, including:
  - One roll each of shiny, crepe, and tissue paper
  - A box of colored pipe cleaners
  - Three fuzzy or foam balls
  - One box of at least sixty-four crayons
  - One container of glitter
  - One roll of double-sided transparent tape

Procedure

1. Place the scissors and glue sticks on each table before the session begins and let participants select their own supplies from a centrally located supply table.

2. Divide participants into small groups of four to seven people each.

3. Describe the issue or opportunity that brings the group together. For instance, "We are here to answer the question, 'What does a team look like?'" or "What does our customer satisfaction look like?" (Surprise is an essential element, so do not reveal the procedure beforehand.)

4. Have each subgroup select a theme (for example, improving a business unit's customer satisfaction). Ask the groups to discuss their themes when things are going well (for example, a vision of success, a desired end-state, a success in another situation) and to call out descriptive adjectives (for example, "Open!" "Fun!" "Trusting!"). Have one member of each group record those adjectives on the flipchart so all group members can see them.

5. Invite each participant to express his or her image of the theme individually, using any of the art supplies. Tell participants they may talk, but should work independently on their own designs. Turn on some appropriate music and let them enjoy working! After 5 or 10 minutes, signify a shift. Stop the music. Get everyone's attention and say, "Everyone please stand up and move one seat to the right and begin working on the design there." Begin the music again.

6. After 5 minutes, turn the music down again, get everyone's attention, and instruct them to stand up and move one seat to the right again. Begin the music again. After another 5 minutes, turn the music down and provide one more instruction to move to the right. This time, though, say: "Shift happens. Watch what I do and duplicate my actions with the project in front of you."

7. Take an 8 ½" x 11" piece of paper, tear it in half horizontally, and then tear it vertically. This leaves four pieces of paper. Say, "Now I'd like you to do the same and rearrange the four pieces into a new expression of the design's theme. Rearrange the four pieces so some jagged edges are on the outside and some straight pieces are adjacent in the middle." (*Note:* Never have anyone tear up a piece they have contributed to themselves and be sure there are more people at each table than there are rotations.)

8. As they rearrange their pieces, invite them to ask the piece what its name is. Sample responses might include, "My name is team unity!" or "My name is team communication!"

9. Complete the activity with a gallery showing. Have each person hold up the piece they LAST worked on (having rearranged the four pieces). Invite as many people as time allows to introduce a piece to the group, mention its name, and describe how it represents the theme.

Discussion

To debrief the activity, ask the participants to discuss the following questions:

- How did that go for you?
- What were your feelings the first time I asked you to shift?
- How did that change the second time? The third time?
- What insights have you gained from the images you have created?
- What insights have you gained from the process?
- What do these insights have to do with the theme at hand?
- How might you apply what you learned to team collaboration?
- How important are perceptual shifts in groups? Why?
- Audre Lorde wrote, "The master's tools will not dismantle the master's house." How does that apply here, in your teams, and the organization?
- Pablo Picasso said, "Every act of creation is first of all an act of destruction." What needs to be done here to ready us for the changes we want to make?
- How might you apply those insights in the workplace?
- What will you do differently when you get back to work tomorrow?

Sources

Lorde, A. (1984). *Sister outsider*. Trumansberg, NY: The Crossing Press.

Picasso, P. www.creativequotations.com/one/11.htm

Contributor

Jan Nickerson transforms ideas into participative learning experiences, tools, and practices. Formerly a CFO of Internet-type businesses and non-profits, she focuses her consulting practice on creative collaboration and self-organizing innovation. Passionate about co-creating in cyberspace, Nickerson has added e-learning environments, tools, and practices to her work with progressive organizations.

6 Drawing

- Commentated Pictures
- Drawing You into Conversation
- Metaphorical Thinking
- Picture Switcher
- Symbolic Code
- Vision Quest

COMMENTATED PICTURES

Objectives

- To include organizational teams in an idealized design process
- To improve team communication
- To capture, store, categorize, and communicate ideas visually and verbally

Uses

- A media-rich way for teams to express their ideas and thoughts
- An effective way for teams to record and communicate with others over time and distance
- As a part of a needs assessment to provide valuable input to a knowledge archive easily accessible by others

Art Form

Drawing

Time Required

15 minutes

Materials, Handouts, and Equipment

- Two sheets of 8.5" x 11" 24 lb. white paper for each participant
- Felt-tip markers for each participant
- (Optional) A digital recording device with a good microphone and sound-editing software (for example, CakeWalk™), a digital camera, and a computer scanner to scan pictures

Procedure

1. Explain that the purpose of this exercise is to help participants better capture and communicate their ideas and thoughts.
2. Give them paper and drawing instruments. Tell them that they will be drawing a picture of an idea, future state, or thing. For instance, "Draw and comment on a picture that represents one or more characteristics of 'ideal' communication in your team."

3. Show them a sample picture. As an example, you might show a picture described as follows:

   "A department or division manager with an elephant's ears stands atop a triangle (representing the company). Two curved arrows, each with a head at both ends, run between the top and the bottom of each side of the triangle linking the manager with the front-line associates. These arrows represent communication from the top of the company to the bottom, from the bottom of the company to the top, and within intact work teams. Also, there are many smiling faces along the bottom of the triangle."

4. Explain what the picture represents. For instance:

   "My picture represents 'ideal' communication: In this picture, our manager has elephant ears, indicating an ability to hear, remember, and act on the many salient ideas, needs, and concerns of our clients and of our front-line associates. The arrows go both ways to reflect the importance of the strategic message that flows from our manager to our front-line employees and from the employees to the manager. The smiling faces represent reps who are highly motivated by the trust that they share in their manager and who feel trusted by the manager and other staff. The smiling faces also represent clients who interact with our motivated front-line associates."

5. Have the participants think for a few minutes about their challenge and then ask them to draw, individually, their pictures and prepare comments about their pictures to present to the group.

6. After everyone has finished drawing their pictures, have them individually describe each one to the group. (Optional: Use the recording device to capture these descriptions, the camera to take photographs of them, and the scanner to store the pictures digitally.)

Discussion

Use the following questions to guide a discussion:

- How did creating the pictures and discussing them with the group help to clarify your visions? What did you like most?
- What was most difficult to do?
- What did you learn from other participants' sharing their pictures?
- How well do you think these "knowledge objects" will describe your thoughts and ideas to others?

Contributor

James Barnes is a creativity consultant who specializes in using innovative thinking processes to enhance teamwork on large projects and corporate change initiatives. He also is founder of YouthStormers, a group of high school and college-age creatives who apply their unfettered minds to corporate issues. He has worked with such clients as Wyeth, Capital One, Whitbread, and Verizon.

DRAWING YOU INTO CONVERSATION

Objectives

- To create rapport between pairs of people
- To provide participants an awareness of the dynamics of conversation and of their customary conversational patterns

Uses

- Icebreaker
- Communication
- Warm-up
- Team building

Art Form

Drawing

Time Required

10 to 20 minutes

Materials, Handouts, and Equipment

- One piece of flipchart paper or plain white paper for each pair of participants
- A different color marker for each member of the pair

Procedure

1. Ask participants to form pairs.
2. Give each participant a different color marker than his or her partner.
3. Position the pair on opposite sides of a piece of paper.
4. Explain that the purpose of the exercise is to have a conversation with your partner via marks on the paper. Tell the participants that they are not to talk during this activity.
5. Demonstrate a simple "conversation" of a few quick abstract lines or shapes (no words). Emphasize that the conversation is the point; the end product is but a "roadmap" of the conversation. Note that there are no right or wrong roadmaps.

6. Instruct the participants to begin drawing.

7. When the "conversations" seem complete (that is, when the energy winds down), call a halt.

8. Debrief using the points below.

9. (Optional) Display the finished conversations for all to see.

Discussion

Discussion questions for debriefing include the following:

- Who made the first mark?

- Is this typical of your verbal conversational style?

- Did you and your partner converse mostly in abstract lines or in symbols? What do any differences signify?

- Did you both stay clear of your partner's marks, or did you interact on the paper—circling, crossing over, or changing your partner's marks? If so, how did your partner react?

- Were there any impulses you censored? If so, what reaction did you fear from your partner that caused you to hold back?

- How do you feel about the conversation you just had? Was it satisfying, frustrating, some of both?

- What did you wish you could say or ask your partner during the exercise?

- In what ways was your behavior during this exercise typical of your usual conversational style?

- What implications do your answers have for team communication?

Variation

This exercise can also be done with small groups gathered around larger pieces of paper. Each participant in the group should have a different color marker. This variation is particularly useful for icebreaking or team building with group members who do not share a common, spoken language.

Contributor

Jacquie Lowell, M.Ed., has been leading creativity and improvisational comedy workshops for twenty-five years. Drawing on experience in theater, dance, psychology, and metaphysics, she has developed lively creativity-stimulating exercises and training programs for companies, organizations, conferences, and schools. She also directs the "Creative Urges" and "Mission Improvible" improvisational comedy troupes.

METAPHORICAL THINKING

Objectives

- To use metaphors to improve team performance
- To provide practice in framing problems

Uses

- Warm-up
- Creative thinking
- Communications

Art Forms

- Drawing
- Storytelling

Time Required

30 to 60 minutes

Materials, Handouts, and Equipment

- One marker and a pen or pencil per participant
- Three sheets of bond paper for each participant
- A collection of pictures cut from magazines, at least twenty pictures per group

Procedure

1. Divide participants into small groups of four to seven people each.

2. Ask participants, "What is a metaphor?" and lead a brief discussion about it. Offer definitions such as those from Aristotle: "The greatest thing by far is to be a master of metaphor. It is a sign of genius, since a good metaphor implies an intuitive perception of the similarity in dissimilars" (*Poetics*) and from Kenneth Burke: "A metaphor is a device for seeing something in terms of something else."

3. Offer examples of metaphors:

"Memory is a crazy woman that hoards colored rags and throws away food."—Austin O'Malley

"Men are from Mars, women are from Venus, and children are from Heaven."—John Gray

4. Say to the participants:

    "Metaphors are vehicles for simplifying complexity and revealing the essence of concepts meaningful to receivers. Metaphors help us capture the essence of current reality and see it in new ways. We use metaphors to describe an ideal, gain insights into solving problems, or to help sell ideas."

5. Tell the participants to think of a work group situation or topic (for example, role expectations, communication, decision making).

6. Have them describe this topic or situation as a metaphor. Say:

    "What image comes to mind when you think of this situation or topic? For instance, communication might evoke an image of spider webs."

7. Give everyone paper and markers and a pen or pencil and instruct them to draw pictures of their images and then convert the images to words or phrases.

8. After everyone has completed their drawings, ask them to share their metaphors with their groups, select one or two favorites, and then share them with members of any other groups.

Discussion

Lead a discussion using the following questions:

- How easy or difficult was it to think metaphorically?

- What was your favorite metaphor?

- What did you learn from this exercise in general and about team collaboration in particular?

- How can using metaphors enhance your teamwork?

- Will using metaphors help your work group solve problems more creatively? Why or why not? Are some problems more appropriate for this type of activity? If so, which ones?

Variation

Ask participants to think of a dream they've had recently. Have them consider whether there might be a connection between their dreams and situations they are dealing with in real life. In what ways could the dream be a metaphor for a particular work situation? Have everyone who chooses to do so tell their dreams and try to apply them to their work team or organization.

Contributor

Linda Naiman, BFA, works with organizations to awaken genius-level thinking through the art and science of applying creativity, innovation, and visionary thinking to business strategy. Naiman is a life-long artist and presents workshops on creativity and innovation in North America and Europe.

PICTURE SWITCHER

Objectives

- To enhance creative thinking abilities
- To increase team self-esteem and confidence
- To demonstrate the importance of teamwork

Uses

- Team building
- Problem solving
- New product development
- Warm-ups

Art Form

Drawing

Time Required

60 to 90 minutes

Materials, Handouts, and Equipment

- Ten sheets of 8.5" x 11" blank paper per participant
- At least two sharpened pencils per participant

Procedure

1. Organize the participants into small groups of three to seven people each.

2. Briefly describe the stages of the four-step "TILS" process that apply to this exercise:

    - Think-it (create an outline)
    - Ink-it (add undertones)
    - Link-it (add other elements)
    - Sync-it (add final details)

3. *Think-it.* Ask each person to draw a simplified sketch of a mountain scene, first creating a box frame with a dot in the center (to help center their perspective). Tell them that artistic ability is not important. However, they should think about what a mountain scene looks like to them and draw it to the best of their ability.

4. This first sketch should be signed, dated, and hidden from the team until later.

5. Tell the groups they will now be creating a team picture.

6. *Ink-it.* Instruct each person to reproduce his or her first sketch, then to switch pictures with a teammate and to work individually to add to their neighbors' pictures. (Note that to shade, they can use the side of their lead pencil and vary the pressure to depict light, medium, and dark undertones.)

7. Tell them to stop and switch papers again, but with another group member.

8. *Link-it.* Instruct everyone to add elements that might be in a mountain scene and to continue switching papers periodically. For instance, tall tree trunks or a fence could be drawn in the front. Tiny trees along the bottom of the distant area could link the big front trees to balance the picture. Do not let them overdo this step; ask them to keep it simple.

9. Tell them to stop and switch papers for the last time.

10. *Sync-it.* This final step of the TILS process involves adding details. These could be a barren tree with branches and twigs, a cabin in the distance, weeds, grass, et cetera. Again, it's better to keep the picture simple.

11. The final step of the exercise is to compare each individual's original mountain picture with those produced by the team.

Discussion

Lead a discussion using the following questions:

- What added value can people receive from working as a team versus working alone?

- How important is coordination during team collaboration?

- How important is respect for everyone's ideas and cultural differences?

- How can different points of view and past art experiences enhance team collaboration? How can they inhibit it?

- What do you learn by interacting with others during this activity?
- What examples from your personal experiences might illustrate some of the points brought out in this activity?

Contributor

Conni Gordon, CSP (certified speaking professional), is known as an entertaining educator. Recognized in the *Guinness Book of World Records* as the "World's Most Prolific Teacher of Creative Art," she has developed and patented a four-step method (the TILS teaching technique) to create instant art and has applied it to business problem solving. She is the co-author (with Richard Israel) of *How To THINK Creatively Using the Conni Gordon "TILS" 4-Step Technique.*

SYMBOLIC CODE

Objectives

- To improve symbolic thinking
- To help teams use symbolic thinking to solve problems

Uses

- Values clarification
- Nonverbal communication
- Intercultural communication
- Creative thinking
- Group identity

Art Forms

- Abstraction
- Drawing/illustration

Time Required

2 hours

Materials, Handouts, and Equipment

One each of the following for each participant:

- Pioneer F Plaque Symbology handout
- Pencils
- Colored markers
- Piece of bond paper

Procedure

1. Divide participants into subgroups of four to seven members each.
2. Read the following aloud:

"Egyptian hieroglyphics are perhaps one of the most well-known examples of symbolic language. The Pioneer F Plaque outer space program is another. It is designed to communicate to intelligent life on other planets and to indicate that we have intelligent life on our planet. Scientists currently are decoding the genome and mapping intelligent life of humans at the cellular level. Consequently, DNA has become another popular metaphor for mapping organizational intelligence. As Agnes Denes notes: 'Pattern recognition, mapping, sequencing, decoding and visualizing make up the language of genetics. Finding invisible patterns, interpreting and applying the results is what the Genome Project is all about. When arts renders into visual form these analytical processes, the hybrid becomes the script in a new language of seeing and knowing: a summation and dramatization of new associations and analogies. The powerful tools of this new science can thus be enhanced by the equally powerful tools of artistic vision, image and metaphor, which become expressions of human values with profound impact on our consciousness and collective destiny.'" ("Evolution and the Creative Mind," *Art Journal,* Spring 1996, College Arts Association)

3. Invite their comments and lead a discussion about symbols as a form of communication within work teams.

4. Distribute copies of the handout and have the participants look at the picture of the Pioneer F Plaque and see whether they can decipher the meaning of the code *before they read the description*. Then have them read the description and ask questions or make comments.

5. Instruct each group to write code describing their team in general or a team project. This code should be in the form of visual symbols and not words. The objective is to communicate symbolically to the non-English speaking world (this one or beyond!). Tell them to include in this code who they are, what they stand for, and what their mission is. Remember, no words.

6. Tell each group to display its code on the wall and have the other groups try to decipher it.

Discussion

Discuss what you learned from this exercise using the following questions as guides:

- What do these codes say about you as individuals? About you as work groups?
- How well did your group make itself understood?
- How effective were your symbols as a means of communication?
- How well could your group decipher other codes? To what degree were you able to use each other's interpretations as a springboard for finding clues?
- What insights did you get from other people's symbols?
- What have you learned about art in relation to science?
- How might art and science be used together to improve team collaboration?
- How does this exercise enhance communication, cultural awareness, group identity, community building, or knowledge creation and management?

Contributor

Linda Naiman, BFA, works with organizations to awaken genius-level thinking through the art and science of applying creativity, innovation, and visionary thinking to business strategy. Naiman is a life-long artist and presents workshops on creativity and innovation in North America and Europe.

Pioneer F Plaque Symbology

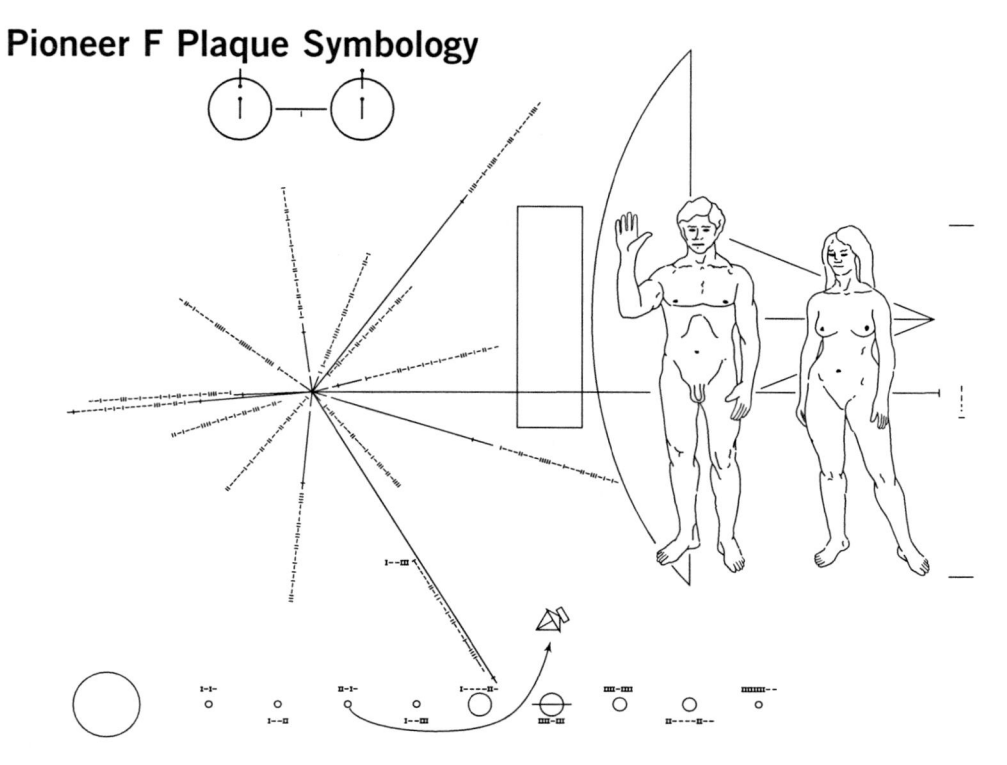

The Pioneer F spacecraft, destined to be the first manmade object to escape from the solar system into interstellar space, carries the pictorial plaque shown above. It is designed to show scientifically educated inhabitants of some other star system, who might intercept it millions of years from now, when Pioneer was launched, from where, and by what kind of beings. (With the hope that they would not invade Earth.)

The radiating lines at left represent the positions of fourteen pulsars, a cosmic source of radio energy, arranged to indicate our sun as the home star of our civilization. The "1-" symbols at the ends of the lines are binary numbers that represent the frequencies of these pulsars at the time of launch of Pioneer F relative to that of the hydrogen atom shown at the upper left with a "1" unity symbol. The hydrogen atom is thus used as a "universal clock," and the regular decrease in the frequencies of the pulsars will enable another civilization to determine the time that has elapsed since Pioneer F was launched.

The hydrogen is also used as a "universal yardstick" for sizing the human figures and outline of the spacecraft shown on the right. The hydrogen wavelength, about 8 inches, multiplied by the binary number representing "8" shown next to the woman gives her height, 64 inches. The figures represent the type of creature that created Pioneer. The man's hand is raised in a gesture of good will.

Across the bottom are the planets, ranging outward from the Sun, with the spacecraft trajectory arching away from Earth, passing Mars, and swinging by Jupiter.

Source: NASA, Center Number: 72-H-192, GRIN DataBase Number: GPN-2000–001623

VISION QUEST

Objectives

- To create a common vision that captures the aspirations of a group, team, or organization
- To explore the meaning that underlies a vision for the future

Uses

- Leadership and management training
- Visioning
- Team building

Art Forms

- Drawing
- Painting
- Storytelling

Time Required

45 minutes to 2 hours, depending on group size

Materials, Handouts, and Equipment

- Flipchart and paper
- At least one piece of paper (11" x 17" or 18" x 24") per participant
- Pens, markers, crayons, or paint brushes, paint, and containers of water for each participant

Procedure

1. Explain that you will take people on a "vision quest" (a guided visualization) to help gain insight into the future. Note that while the rational mind is important, "We gain a new perspective when we learn how many of the greatest scientific insights, discoveries, and revolutionary inventions appeared first to their creators as fantasies, dreams, trances, lightening-flash insights, and other non-ordinary states of consciousness," according to Willis Harman and Howard Rheingold (*Higher Creativity.* New York: Tarcher/Putnam, 1984).

2. Say that the experience of expanded states of consciousness has been remarkably similar among artists, composers, and poets as well as scientists. Kekule, famous for his dream-inspired scientific breakthrough (discovery of the molecular structure of benzene), advised his fellow scientists: "Let us learn to dream, gentlemen."

3. Read the following instructions slowly and calmly:

   "Sit in a comfortable position, get quiet, relax, close your eyes, and breathe deeply. Gather your thoughts and let go of any mind chatter, any worries that take you out of the present moment. With each breath you take, you relax even more, your emotions are calm, and your mind is still. From this place of calm and quiet, sink deep into the essence of your being and imagine you are a very wise sage who has come to this planet to offer your services. Think about how you can best use your gifts and talents in relation to your work, community, and the world. What are the best possible futures for your team or organization?"

4. Tell them to feel free to modify or ask other questions. Allow a few minutes of silence for this activity. End the visualization by softly instructing people to return to their bodies, stretch, and when they are ready, open their eyes.

5. Give them materials and have them paint or draw in silence their desired future using metaphoric pictures or symbols, but no words.

6. Tell them to form groups of four and create a group vision. Discuss their individual visions. Remind them to include in their stories the emotions, characters, plots, and meanings of their symbols and metaphors. Once everyone has told his or her story, discuss key differences and similarities. What insights might they have gained?

7. Mount all the pictures on a wall and have each group report on key themes and emerging patterns of their visions. They also should report any differences.

8. Collect the themes, differences, and similarities in the entire group's visions for further discussion.

Discussion

Use the following questions to help guide the discussion:

- What common themes have emerged from the group?
- What seem to be the emerging stories?
- What implications are there for team collaboration?
- What is the meaning and significance of the differences?
- What is the next step for team members? For the team as a whole?

Contributor

Linda Naiman, BFA, works with organizations to awaken genius-level thinking through the art and science of applying creativity, innovation, and visionary thinking to business strategy. Naiman is a life-long artist and presents workshops on creativity and innovation in North America and Europe.

7 Music

- Bamboos
- Group Groove
- Jazzin' It

BAMBOOS

Objectives

- To raise awareness of listening and co-creation skills in a fun and creative activity
- To build leadership confidence
- To encourage creative responses to situations

Uses

- Team building
- Nonverbal communication
- Trust building

Art Forms

- Theater
- Music

Time Required

20 to 30 minutes

Materials, Handouts, and Equipment

- Two bamboo sticks for each person, each stick being about one-half inch wide and four feet long.

Procedure

1. Have groups of seven to ten participants stand in circles. Everyone should be wearing shoes.
2. Give each person a bamboo stick.
3. Tell people to hold their sticks about two-thirds of the way up using their right hands.
4. Tell participants that you will count down from three. When you get to zero, you want them to throw their bamboo sticks to the right, so that they drop vertically in front of the person to their right.

5. Caution them to look directly in front of them, not to the side, and trust that they will be able to catch the stick thrown to them from their left.

6. Try to establish a rhythm. Some people will drop the bamboo and laugh. When that happens, wait for them to pick up their sticks and start the next countdown.

7. Begin the activity by counting down from three. Whenever someone drops a stick, wait in silence for him or her to pick it up. As the participants become more proficient, reduce the countdown from three to two, then to one, and then just allow the rhythm to determine the passing. (At this point, when someone drops a stick, announce that there will be no countdown.)

8. After another round or two, introduce the second stick, so that each person now is holding two.

9. Tell them to throw from their right hand, pass the second stick from their left to their right hand, and catch the incoming bamboo with their now empty left hand. The trick is not to think about it, but just to trust that it will work.

Discussion

Creating a rhythm and flow can take time. Participants soon learn that forcing does not help. They also learn that you must wait for everyone to be settled and concentrating before a round can start. Once "flow" is achieved, a magic meditation moment seems to occur when all the sticks are flowing harmoniously around the group. A soft, relaxed concentration allows this to happen.

A short debriefing allows people to express the importance of concentration, relaxing, and trusting. The real message lies in the experience. Some questions to ask following this activity include:

- What happened? Tell the story of the exercise.
- What did you notice about when it worked best and when it did not?
- What was the difference in your attitude?
- What was the difference in the group?
- How did the energy in the group change?
- What did you discover from participating in this activity?
- How can you relate this activity to your work life?

Contributor

Tim Merry is a partner in Engage! InterAct, an organization that encourages people to look to the benefits of difference and diversity and that helps them work together to promote and celebrate the values of respect, cooperation, and creativity. The group engages with youth, commercial, nonprofit, and governmental organizations.

GROUP GROOVE

Objectives

- To help people relax and focus before a meeting
- To help a group of people get in sync with one another
- To build community

Uses

- Team building
- Risk taking
- Communication

Art Form

Music

Time Required

10 to 15 minutes

Materials, Handouts, and Equipment

- A CD of upbeat, lively music (check copyright restrictions)
- A CD player
- An egg shaker (purchased or home made) for each participant

Procedure

1. Purchase or make shakers. Shakers can be made from empty soda pop cans. Beans or rice can be placed in them and the openings sealed over with tape. Experiment with the amount and kind of grain or legume placed inside for a sound that pleases you. (Constructing shakers can be a great team-building exercise by itself. Egg shakers can be purchased at most music stores or can be ordered directly at 800–930–8812.)

2. Have the participants assemble into groups of five to twenty, preferably standing.

3. Designate one person in each group to keep the beat.

4. Distribute an egg shaker to each participant, direct the beat keeper to begin shaking his or her shaker, and tell the other members of the group to shake their shakers in sync with the beat keeper.

5. Once a group begins to shake together, tell participants that anyone in the group can comment on how they are doing. Are they holding the rhythm steady? Or is the group starting to accelerate? This is a mysterious process. Who controls the rhythm? Where do changes in the system come from? Can they be localized or is a change in tempo a systemic phenomenon? Is regulation subject to conscious control? How can members who are better at regulating tempo help the others who may have a tendency to speed up or show down? In this way, the group begins to explore ways that they can support one another.

6. Start the CD. Tell participants that they should shake their shakers and find the underlying pulse of the music playing in the background. (Use a piece that is about 4 or 5 minutes long at a constant medium tempo—not super fast or slow.) Explain to the participants that the goal is to relax and focus on listening to how closely individuals are keeping to the "underlying groove" as well as opening up to the entire group. The tendency is to stay insulated or solo when we learn new competencies, especially in front of colleagues. Simultaneously practicing staying centered in our own rhythm, while opening up to the collective energy of the group, becomes a powerful metaphor for balancing individual roles, skills, and the group's rhythm for learning as individuals and as a collective.

7. Next, say that if someone becomes too focused on "getting it," other team members can remind him or her to relax and breathe. Staying in the groove is, paradoxically, possible only by being able and willing to fall out and stop when members get out of sync. This process of starting and stopping over again is good practice for allowing mistakes to happen.

8. After the song is over, ask the groups to try to maintain a steady rhythm on their own.

9. After a few minutes, say, "Let's gradually fade into silence." Ask participants to try to fade out at the same rate, gradually diminishing their volume level until the shakers are silent.

Discussion

After shaking up a storm, have the entire group sit down and contemplate the following questions:

- What did you notice about this exercise in terms of music or rhythms?
- What seemed easy or challenging for you?
- What factors influenced your ability to stay in sync with one another?
- What kinds of words or actions seemed to help?
- Which words or actions made it more difficult for you?
- What principles can you see at work here in terms of finding your rhythm individually and collectively? What are they and how might they apply to working together?
- How might each of you be supportive of one another's learning so that you can raise the performance level of your team?
- How else might you apply learnings from this exercise to your work together?

Contributor

Performing artist, educator, and facilitator Gary Muszynski is a pioneer in the field of experiential learning. His broad musical experience and his unique ability to apply the principles of music to other areas have earned him recognition as an active contributor to the fields of music, group facilitation, and organizational development.

JAZZIN' IT

Objectives

- To help individuals think quickly on their feet
- To enhance higher order thinking skills
- To improve decision-making skills

Uses

- Presentation skills
- Fast thinking
- Creative thinking

Art Form

Music

Time Required

60 to 90 minutes

Materials, Handouts, and Equipment

- An assortment of rhythm instruments (or common household or office items that can be used as music instruments, for example, pencil sharpener, ballpoint pen with ridges on its casing, a chair, a clipboard, a spiral notebook, pots and pans, spoons)
- Paper and pencils for each participant

Procedure

1. Assemble participants into groups of four to five people and distribute paper and pencils.

2. Distribute an assortment of instruments (or items to be used as instruments) so members of each subgroup have different instruments.

3. Instruct the participants to find three distinct sounds that each item can make. If possible, find soft, medium, and loud sounds with each representing a different type of sound.

4. Have them designate on paper a symbol for each of the sounds.

5. Ask them to write a sixteen-symbol song with the symbols they created.

6. Have each musician rehearse his or her composition. Tell them to practice simultaneously, working to block out the other musicians and concentrate on their own pieces.

7. Ask the participants to perform their piece, solo, for their groups. This should take place throughout the room, with one soloist performing at a time within each subgroup.

8. After each solo, have the participant pass his or her piece and instrument to another member of the group and ask that person to play his or her colleague's piece for a different interpretation of the composition. Afterward, the person should return the instrument and music to the first person.

9. After all the participants have had a chance to perform for their subgroups, ask each subgroup to perform their pieces together as an ensemble. This will provide new textures to the music and change the nature of the songs. (They first should rehearse among themselves and then perform for the large group.)

10. Ask all of the groups to play their pieces simultaneously while you act as the conductor. This texture will be a "sound tapestry," weaving all the patterns and themes of each person's contributions.

Discussion

Lead a discussion using the following questions:

- Did you find it difficult to practice while others were practicing? Why or why not?
- How did you feel about performing for your group?
- How did you feel when someone else played your composition?
- How can what you learned here by applied to team communication?

Contributor

Janice Kilgore has varied experiences in the professional music world as well as being a devout music educator and musician. She was trained at the University of North Texas with degrees in music education (B.M., M.M.E.). She is currently working on a doctorate at UNT in creative thinking through music education applications. She has served as a consultant and lecturer since 1987 and is in over ten editions of *Who's Who*, including *Who's Who in Entertainment*. Ms. Kilgore has created a distance learning music education program for children and contributed to several exercises in *101 Great Games and Activities* (Pfeiffer). She is currently on staff at Tarrant County College, Southeast Campus, as a music instructor.

8 Painting

- Getting Graphic
- Spheres of Influence
- Visual Symphonies

GETTING GRAPHIC

Objectives

- To use visuals to clarify challenges
- To illustrate current reality
- To develop metaphors and symbols
- To analyze a problem

Uses

- Creative problem solving
- Communication
- Clarifying expectations

Art Forms

- Painting
- Drawing
- Graphic design

Time Required

Approximately 60 minutes

Materials, Handouts, and Equipment

- A variety of poster or tempera paint of different colors for each group
- One sheet of white flipchart paper per group
- One table with chairs per group
- One easel per group (optional)
- ½" to 1" wide paint brushes for each participant
- Containers for paint and water (or colored markers) for each group

Procedure

1. Divide participants into small groups of four to five people seated at small tables. Ideally, the participants would represent natural work groups, although this is not required.

2. Have the small groups brainstorm important group challenges.

3. Ask the groups to generate ideas for metaphors and symbols that express the essence of their issues or challenges. For instance, they might describe someone fishing as a metaphor for identifying new markets. (For more information, refer to Metaphorical Thinking in Chapter 6.)

4. Have each group design and illustrate a poster. Tell them to divide up tasks so that one person writes headlines, others draw the images, and still others paint the images.

5. Collect the posters and put them on a wall to make a mural.

6. Instruct the participants to browse among the posters, make notes, and then discuss observations with the large group.

7. Tell each group to use information gleaned from any of the posters as triggers for ideas to deal with the group's challenge.

Discussion

Have the participants discuss such questions as:

- What ideas resulted from using your posters?
- How important was verbal communication during this exercise? Why was that?
- How effectively were emotions conveyed in the posters?
- What effects have you created?
- What are the meanings, context, and insights revealed by your posters?
- Did any deeper issues emerge? If so, what were they?
- As a large group, what are the most important issues?

Contributor

Linda Naiman, BFA, works with organizations to awaken genius-level thinking through the art and science of applying creativity, innovation, and visionary thinking to business strategy. Naiman is a life-long artist and presents workshops on creativity and innovation in North America and Europe.

SPHERES OF INFLUENCE

Objectives

- To develop creative team collaboration
- To develop symbolic and metaphoric expression
- To develop self-awareness and group awareness

Uses

- Design and implementation
- Collaboration
- Community building

Art Forms

- Painting
- Multimedia

Time Required

Approximately 2 hours

Materials, Handouts, and Equipment

- Two sheets of bond paper per person
- A collection of random full-page pictures cut from magazines (one picture per group)
- Enough painting and drawing supplies (paint, brushes, pens, pencils, markers) for participants to have one of each

Procedure

1. Tell participants the objective is to create an art piece based on the theme, "Spheres of Influence." As an example, tell them that in 1986, artist Tony Oursler created an installation called Spheres of Influence at the Musée National d'Art Moderne in Paris. He suspended large spheres from the ceiling of a room and arranged spheres on the floor as well. Some of the spheres were illuminated by a video on a tripod that projected words and images onto the screens.

2. Organize the participants into groups of four (ideally, natural work units). Have each person think about the spheres of influence on their work teams. Suggest that sources of influence might include books, film, TV, teachers, critics, art, conferences, et cetera. Have them consider the five Ws—Who? What? When? Why? Where?—and How? in their discussions. For instance, "Who influences them most in their teams? Why were they influenced?" Also ask them to think about how they are spheres of influence themselves. That is, whom do they influence?

3. Tell them to write down their spheres of influence.

4. Give everyone paper and art supplies. Ask each participant to draw or paint symbolic or metaphoric representations of his or her spheres of influence. (For instance, one metaphor might be a magnet or a force field.)

5. Within subgroups, have everyone show their pictures and discuss them.

6. Give each person a randomly chosen picture from a magazine. Tell them to think about how they could become a more powerful sphere of influence as a group by making a connection between the picture and their task. For instance, "What metaphor or symbol does the picture evoke?" If the picture was an oracle, what message does it hold for the group?

7. Instruct the groups to decide which interpretations work best and have one person from each group draw or paint a new image.

8. Ask all the groups to reconvene and share their pictures and stories.

Discussion

Lead a discussion using the following questions:

- How do spheres of influence affect you?
- What are you most influenced by? Why? Least influenced by? Why?
- In what ways are you a sphere of influence?
- What have you learned from each other and from your own process?
- What meanings can you extract from the images you have created?
- Do the images add to your awareness of the group and of yourself?
- What patterns did you see emerging?
- Could these images be code for an emerging story and future possibilities for your team?
- What possibilities do you see for being more effective as a group?

Contributor

Linda Naiman, BFA, works with organizations to awaken genius-level thinking through the art and science of applying creativity, innovation, and visionary thinking to business strategy. Naiman is a life-long artist and presents workshops on creativity and innovation in North America and Europe.

VISUAL SYMPHONIES

Objectives

- To develop symbolic thinking
- To express what is difficult to express
- To awaken senses and explore new ways of creating

Uses

- Nonverbal communication
- Listening
- Icebreaker
- Warm-up
- Creative thinking

Art Forms

- Painting
- Music

Time Required

1 to 2 hours

Materials, Handouts, and Equipment

- A classical music CD and player
- A projector to show a web page on screen (or screen shots on an overhead transparency or computer printouts for each participant)
- One computer with Internet access (optional)
- For each participant:
  - A variety of paint colors (water color, tempera, or children's poster paints)
  - Five sheets of paper (approximately 18" x 24")
  - One paint brush
  - Containers for paint, if needed (plastic ice cube trays will do)

- One container of water
- Paper towels

Procedure

1. Prior to the session, choose a piece of classical music for participants to listen to. Suggested composers include Mozart, Beethoven, Stravinsky, Janacek, Smetana, and Dvorak. As a contrast, try contemporary composers such as Cage or Sakamoto. Be sure not to violate any copyright restrictions.

2. Divide the participants into groups of four.

3. Read this quote by the painter Wassily Kandinsky (1866–1944), who was the first to "paint music" and to create truly abstract art:

"A painter who finds no satisfaction in mere representation, however artistic, in his longing to express his inner life, cannot but envy the ease with which music, the most non-material of the arts today, achieves this end."

4. Tell them Kandinsky's interest in the expression of the soul led him to explore the relationship between art and music. (It has been said by many that music, light, and color make up the language of the soul.) Say,

"Kandinsky revolutionized the art world through his spiritual quest to express inner feeling rather than outer reality in his paintings of music. His book, Concerning the Spiritual in Art (1914) is considered the most influential treatise on art theory of the 20th Century—and has impacted the development of *all* abstract art since."

5. Start playing the classical music and instruct participants to listen with their eyes closed and imagine the shapes and colors of the music.

6. Hand out the supplies. Play the music again, but this time have participants paint what they hear.

7. (Optional) Show examples of Kandinsky's paintings from www.ibiblio.org/wm/paint/auth/kandinsky. Be sure to show participants Kandinsky's paintings after they have created their paintings. This will ensure all express their unique experiences of the music they are listening to.

8. Put the paintings on the wall to display and have the participants discuss them.

Discussion

Use the following questions to guide a discussion:

- How easy was it to see what you were hearing?
- What are the similarities and differences in your pictures?
- Did you learn something new about thinking and perceiving with your senses?
- Were you able to tap into the expression of emotional experience that is often too subtle for words?
- What are your thoughts about music and art being the language of the soul?
- Did you learn something new about other members of your group?
- Can you see a relationship between composition in music, painting, and orchestrating collaboration in organizations?
- How well do you stop and "listen to the whole" as an individual within a group when you collaborate?
- Can you listen for what is trying to emerge from your collaborative process? What other implications are there for team performance?
- What other implications are there for team collaboration or performance?
- What did this activity teach you about tacit knowledge and collective knowledge in your team?

Variation

Listen to another composer from a different time period and repeat the above exercise.

Contributor

Linda Naiman, BFA, works with organizations to awaken genius-level thinking through the art and science of applying creativity, innovation, and visionary thinking to business strategy. Naiman is a life-long artist and presents workshops on creativity and innovation in North America and Europe.

9 Poetry

- Limerick Your Learning
- Poetry in Motion
- Rhyme and Reason
- Rhyme Time

LIMERICK YOUR LEARNING

Objectives

- To promote team collaboration
- To provide humor and entertainment for participants
- To help participants anchor what they learned
- To enhance creative thinking skills

Uses

- Team building
- Energizer
- Warm-up

Art Form

Poetry

Time Required

30 to 45 minutes

Materials, Handouts, and Equipment

- One copy of the Limerick Your Learning handout per group
- Paper and a pen or pencil for each group

Procedure

1. Put participants in groups of three to five people.

2. Give one person in each group a copy of the handout, blank paper, and a pen or pencil.

3. Give a brief history of the limerick: This poetry form originated in the town of Limerick in Ireland. Most people associate limericks with dirty verses found on bathroom walls, but the original rhyme scheme was made famous by Shakespeare and has been used for all kinds of humor, verse, and poetry.

4. Describe the rhyme scheme and meter and read out examples in the handout to illustrate.

5. Have each group select a work or training-related topic, such as improving communication.

6. Direct each group to select one person to record ideas.

7. Tell each group to begin creating a limerick that addresses the topic selected. Note that group members should be open to each person's ideas and not jump to judgment.

8. Tell the idea recorders to write down all ideas and, as much as possible, use the lines most people feel happy with. Tell them to allow other people's ideas to enhance theirs. (If necessary, some groups may have to be reminded to keep it PG-rated.)

9. Give each group 10 minutes to create the limericks.

10. Have each group read out its limerick and lead applause afterward.

Discussion

Lead a short discussion using such questions as:

- How effective was collaborating on this limerick?
- What was the process you used? How well did it work?
- How does a process like this affect your learning today?
- Did using the limericks help you better understand training outcomes?

Contributor

Carla Rieger, B.A., C.R.P., is a performance storyteller, trainer, and humorist. She specializes in using theatre, storytelling, and humor to enhance communications within diverse groups. She has over fifteen years of experience in the performing arts. She is the director of YES Education Systems, a creative communications consulting firm, and is the co-founder of the Vancouver Playback Theatre Troupe. She is currently touring her latest solo show, entitled Dancing Between Worlds, that explores the perilous journey of reclaiming one's creative self. Her two manuals, *The Power of Laughter* and *Captivate Your Audience,* promote the use of fun and play in workplace settings. Her work has been featured on radio, TV, and in magazines. As a frequent speaker and performer before all types of business and civic groups internationally, Rieger helps them build bridges both inside and out.

Limerick Your Learning*

_____(A)
(8 syllables)

_____(A)
(8 syllables)

_____(B)
(6 syllables)

_____(B)
(6 syllables)

_____(A)
(8 syllables)

Examples:

1.
A daring young robber named Pratt,
Said, "Put all your cash in my hat,"
To the fast-food cashier,
"Or I'll shoot off your ear!"
Cashier says, "Ya want fries with that?"

2.
Creative discussions are great
When all are willing to debate
Make sure it is safe
Otherwise it will chafe
We want all to participate

3.
To let go of your extra stress
Just go celebrate for success
You will anchor the goods
Balance fun with the shoulds
And give yourself that luxurious rest

---

* Note: All the lines marked "A" are to rhyme with each other and all the lines marked "B" are to rhyme with each other.

Reproduced from *Orchestrating Collaboration at Work* by Arthur B. VanGundy & Linda Naiman with permission of the publisher. Copyright © 2005 by Arthur B. VanGundy & Linda Naiman.

POETRY IN MOTION

Objectives

- To understand the importance of nonverbal communication
- To practice keeping an open mind with new ideas
- To clarify team goals

Uses

- Nonverbal communication
- Team building
- Leadership
- Collaboration and cooperation

Art Form

Poetry

Time Required

45 to 60 minutes

Materials, Handouts, and Equipment

- Sixty sheets of multi-colored cardstock paper, 8.5" x 11", for each group
- One marker for each participant
- Flipchart paper or a notepad for each group

Procedure

1. Prior to the session, prepare for each group fifty sheets of paper with one each of the following words written on them (use block letters about 2 inches to 3 inches tall):

A	MARKETING
ABOUT	MONEY
AN	MOVE
AND	NEAR
APPROVAL	NEED
AROUND	OF
BUDGET	PLAN
COLLABORATION	POWER
COMMUNICATION	PRODUCTS
CONFLICT	REDUCE
CREATE	REPORT
CUSTOMERS	SALES
DECISION	SAY
FALLING	SEE
FROM	SQUEEZE
GOAL	STRESS
HEAR	TABLE
HELP	TALK
IF	TEAM
IN	THE
INCREASING	TO
LEADER	TRUST
LISTENING	TRY
MAKE	UNCERTAIN
MANAGER	WHEN

Leave ten of the sheets blank.

2. Organize participants into small groups of five to seven people. If possible, these groups should correspond to natural work units.

3. Tell them the major purpose of the exercise is to resolve team performance issues nonverbally, as a group, by creating "moving" poems.

4. Place the materials for each group on a large table or on the floor.

5. Instruct each group to brainstorm at least five team issues (for example, leadership, communication, conflict, product goals).

6. Tell the participants in each group to create a "solution poem" by having members select individually one card with a word on it. Tell them that each individual also may select just one of the ten blank cards instead and write his or her own word on it. All the cards together should represent a phrase pertaining to resolution or insight into one of the problems identified previously.

7. After they pick up a sheet, tell them to look at those chosen by others and create a solution poem by walking around and then standing together in a circle holding the sheets so others can see them. Not all cards must be used. For instance, six members might create the phrase, "MAKE-MANAGER-REDUCE-STRESS-AND-CONFLICT."

8. The one rule is that participants must not talk while creating their poems.

9. Have one group member write down the poem on a flipchart or notepad.

10. Tell them to create at least five poems—one for each team issue—and record them in writing, one per flipchart sheet. (Previously used words may be re-used.)

11. Have the participants in each group review the poems and look for common themes (for example, intra-group conflict, poor communication, lack of collaboration, dealing with a budget cut) pertaining to problem issues or solutions.

12. Tell them to spend 10 minutes brainstorming specific solutions to each problem using the poems and then share all solutions with the larger group (if there is more than one small group).

Discussion

Use the following questions to guide a discussion:

- How easy was it to create the solution poems nonverbally? Why?
- What would be at least one advantage of communicating nonverbally for this task?
- How useful were the poems in identifying issues or resolving problems?
- What role did leadership play in this exercise? Were some members more successful than others at persuading the group how to create their poems? Why?
- One purpose of this exercise was to demonstrate how difficult it is to keep an open mind, even with a seemingly irrelevant task. What did you learn from this activity that you could apply to group brainstorming?
- How would you evaluate the quantity and quality of the ideas you generated? Do you think you could have produced the same quantity and quality without having done this exercise (that is, without using the poems)?

Variation

After participants have completed the activity using nonverbal communication, have them do it again, this time allowing them to speak. Then have them compare differences in outcomes from using the two approaches.

Contributor

Arthur VanGundy, Ph.D., works as a creativity consultant, trainer, and facilitator of brainstorming retreats. He is the author of ten books, including *Techniques of Structured Problem Solving, Training Your Creative Mind, Managing Group Creativity, Brain Boosters for Business Advantage,* and *101 Great Games & Activities.* Major clients include Hershey Foods, S.C. Johnson Company, Xerox, Motorola, Sunbeam, Air Canada, Monsanto, Wyeth-Ayerst Pharmaceuticals, and the Singapore government. He also is founder of All Star Minds, a global Internet brainstorming service.

RHYME AND REASON

Objectives

- To capture unconscious symbolic information as processed by your right brain
- To practice using both sides of the brain to find an encoded solution

Uses

- Problem solving
- Identifying underlying issues with other people

Art Form

Poetry

Time Required

30 to 45 minutes

Materials, Handouts, and Equipment

- Pen and paper for each participant

Procedure

1. Divide participants into small groups of four to seven people.
2. Have each group select a problem for which they would like a solution.
3. Tell them to reduce their description of the problem into a short phrase of no more than two or three words.
4. Once the problem is stated, tell the groups to start making rhymes from the problem. Provide the following instructions:

"You have full poetic license. Your rhymes do not have to sound good, follow strict rules of rhyming, or even make sense! Give yourself permission to indulge in word play and free association without inhibition. The only rule is to have fun and continue your poem until you feel a shift, can see a solution, or run out of words."

5. Share some examples of rhymes and interpretations created by individuals in other workshops. (Groups obviously can create them as well.) Note the shift that takes place in the poem after a line or two as the feelings begin to surface.

#1 Problem: Made a mistake

Rhyme: "Big headache, too much at stake, can't seem to get an even break, what to do, it's up to you, take some time to work it through, shake it off, don't let them scoff, 3M's mistake had a big pay off!"

Reason:

This man was remorseful for a mistake he had made that cost his company money. After writing this poem, he realized he was too concerned about what other people thought about this and had not given himself time or permission to work through how it had happened or what benefit might come of it. His final line (about the famous 3M mistake) inspired him to look at how he might capitalize on information gained from his own mistake. This freed him up to become creative again!

#2 Problem: Uncertain future

Rhyme: "Stun curtain unsure, wonder if there is a cure, do they care, I'm not aware, maybe something here is spare, is there a way we all can share, distribute load, find new mode, maybe this is just a goad, to make us work, do they think we shirk, time to talk or maybe take a walk."

Reason:

This woman had not realized consciously the extent of her distrust with her senior management group. She felt something was being hidden (behind the curtain) and recognized that there had been little discussion of solutions or ways to cut costs rather than cut staff. She also realized she was feeling unappreciated and unrecognized for her contribution to the company. She wanted to be more proactive in finding both the truth and a solution, so she decided to have an open discussion with her bosses. If her openness didn't yield positive results, she would have to reconsider her own future with the company. She felt empowered once she decided to take the decision about her future into her own hands.

6. Have the groups review their poems and look for hidden or symbolic meanings and insights. Have them play with their poems until they stimulate new information or a new idea or approach to their problem.

7. Ask the participants to read their problem and poem to the large group. Encourage them to see what ideas or solutions also come from others.

8. Ask each group to share the ideas that resulted from its poem.

Discussion

Use the following questions to guide a discussion:

- What was your overall experience during this exercise?
- Was it easy for you to generate the poems? Difficult? Why?
- Did you notice personal needs and emotions emerge while creating the poems or generating ideas? If so, what were they?
- Did this exercise make it easier to focus on the problem in a less analytical way?
- Did this exercise help bring out individual creativity that otherwise might have been repressed during a conventional brainstorming session?

Contributor

Gael McCool, Ph.D., is a behavioral consultant and teacher in the Vancouver, B.C., area. In her practice, Dr. McCool has consulted with and provided training to such companies as the Walt Disney Company, Johnson & Johnson, and several television networks. She is currently on sabbatical writing a book, *Emotional Accountability*.

RHYME TIME

Objectives

- To reduce role conflict and ambiguity within small groups
- To improve intra-group communication
- To demonstrate the role arts-based creativity can play in groups

Uses

- Clarifying group roles and responsibilities
- Team building
- Creative thinking

Art Form

Poetry

Time Required

45 minutes

Materials, Handouts, and Equipment

- Flipchart
- Markers
- A copy of the Sample Poem handout for each participant
- Paper and pens or pencils for participants
- A photocopy machine (optional)
- Overhead projector and transparencies (optional)

Procedure

1. Divide participants into small groups of four to seven people each.
2. Tell each group to select a problem area for the group, such as reducing role ambiguity or improving intra-group communication. You also may want to assign different problem areas to the groups.

3. Distribute the Sample Poem handout, blank paper, and pens or pencils. Instruct each participant to read the sample poem and use it as a guide to write a series of four-verse stanzas on the selected problem area. Explain that every other line should rhyme. Thus, the last word in line one should rhyme with line three; the last in line two, with line four. Have them write at least three stanzas. Remind them that the objective is not to produce publishable verse; instead, the purpose is to develop stimulus material for creating different perspectives on challenges facing the groups.

4. Suggest that participants consider using one of two approaches to develop their poems. First, try thinking of two words to use as rhymes with two other words. For instance, select the words "day" and "link." Two other words that would rhyme with these would be "say" and "think." Another approach is to write the first two lines and then generate the other lines to rhyme in alternating order. Remind the group members to study the sample poem again if they need help understanding. And remember, there is no "perfect" poem; the process is more important than the output.

5. Have each participant share his or her poem with the rest of his or her subgroup. If resources permit, photocopy enough copies of each poem for the rest of the group to read or have group members write their poems on overhead transparency film and project them for all to see.

6. Tell the group members to use each poem to help trigger a discussion of roles that need to be clarified within the group, communication patterns that need to be improved, or other topics important to the group.

Discussion

Tell the subgroups to use the following questions as discussion guides or use them to lead a large-group discussion:

- Which approach to writing the poems was easier to use—thinking of two words that rhyme or writing the first two lines? Why? What implications do these differences have for team creativity?

- Did some poems trigger more discussion about group process or collaboration than others? If so, why? (For instance, the most "silly" poems often will prompt some of the best insights.)

- What seemed to be the most important factors in prompting discussions? Were there specific words or lines?

- What roles did different team members play during this exercise? Were these roles similar to those they have played in other team situations?

- Would this exercise work as well for teams with diverse cultural backgrounds? Why or why not?

Variation

For each subgroup, have the members develop a poem together and then use the result to trigger discussions.

Contributor

Arthur VanGundy, Ph.D., works as a creativity consultant, trainer, and facilitator of brainstorming retreats. He is the author of ten books, including *Techniques of Structured Problem Solving, Training Your Creative Mind, Managing Group Creativity, Brain Boosters for Business Advantage,* and *101 Great Games & Activities*. Major clients include Hershey Foods, S.C. Johnson Company, Xerox, Motorola, Sunbeam, Air Canada, Monsanto, Wyeth-Ayerst Pharmaceuticals, and the Singapore government. He also is founder of All Star Minds, a global Internet brainstorming service.

Sample Poem

The future looms ever so soon
As our team starts to prepare,
Singing without carrying a tune
Going where others wouldn't dare.

It won't always be easy.
This isn't a simple task
Nor can we be sleazy. . .
That's too much to ask.

But we can be ready
By thinking of who and why. . .
What's that job of Betty?
Whose head is in the sky?

What is it that we do
When things don't go our way?
Can we make it with just two
of us throughout the long day?

If we listen to our peers
Can we expect to understand
And work through our fears
Without taking a stand?

We've got to find a way
To learn what we each do
And not always have to say,
Who the heck are you?

Reproduced from *Orchestrating Collaboration at Work* by Arthur B. VanGundy & Linda Naiman with permission of the publisher. Copyright © 2005 by Arthur B. VanGundy & Linda Naiman.

10 Storytelling

- Exchanging Perspectives
- Fictionalization and Imaginative "Restoryation"
- It's History
- Once Upon a Team
- Stories of Change
- Story Lines
- Story Weaving
- Time Capsule
- To Go Where No Group Has Gone Before

EXCHANGING PERSPECTIVES

Objectives

- To create mutual understanding in a department or between departments
- To create curiosity for others' viewpoints and experiences
- To improve cooperation among team members

Uses

- Change management
- Cooperation
- Communication
- Team building

Art Form

Storytelling

Time Required

60 minutes

Materials, Handouts, and Equipment

- Flipchart for each group
- Markers for each group

Procedure

1. Divide participants into groups of four people each. Use natural work units whenever possible. If your goal is to improve understanding between departments, include as many departments as possible in each group.

2. Ask each group to choose four workplace topics it would like to address (for example, management styles, human resource policies, staff member retention, inter-department communication).

3. Have individuals in each group select one of the four topics and spend 3 minutes reflecting on it, including its history, effects, and contributing factors.

4. Have each person share his or her reflections with the other group members. These reflections should be in the form of a narrative that might describe, for example, the history of an interdepartmental communication problem.

5. Have each person choose a perspective of someone else in the subgroup. Managers should choose the perspective of a staff member.

6. Instruct all four people to prepare to tell their stories from the perspectives they have chosen. For instance, how did the HR manager experience a communication problem? They should do this in pairs within their groups, helping each other by clarifying perspectives. Remind them that they must defend their "character" (that is, provide valid reasons for people to act and react the way they do).

7. Bring every two groups of four together (with one original subgroup designated "A" and the other "B"), so there now are eight people in each group.

8. Explain that each original subgroup of four will share its stories with the rest of the newly formed group of eight.

9. Advise them to begin their stories by saying: "I'll tell you what happened to me. You'll never believe it!" (This will help increase the energy level for telling the stories.) Ask group "A" to tell its stories and the four variations to group B and then have group B share its stories. The subgroups should record on a flipchart any insights gained from the exercise.

Discussion

Use the following questions to guide a discussion either within the small groups or with the large group:

- What did you experience while telling a story from someone else's perspective?
- Was there anything that surprised you?
- What insights did you gain from this activity?
- How important were listening skills during this activity?
- How might these insights be applied to improve group collaboration or performance?

Contributor

Lena Bjørn is an actress, playwright, and storyteller. She is co-founder of The Dacapo Theatre in Denmark. The Dacapo Theatre is a consultancy using theatre and storytelling as basic working methods. The idea of the theatre is to bring art and business together—not only by bringing the arts into business but by developing a consultancy practice in the crossing between the knowledge and practice of consultants and theatre people.

FICTIONALIZATION AND IMAGINATIVE "RESTORYATION"

Objectives

- To help participants develop a new way of thinking about team or organizational issues
- To allow participants to express and discuss important problems

Uses

- Problem solving
- Vision and mission statement development
- Values clarification
- Team development

Art Form

Storytelling

Time Required

1 to 2 hours

Materials, Handouts, and Equipment

- Eight pieces of flipchart paper per group (four for the Fictionalization and four for the Imaginative "Restoryation" activities) with the appropriate headings (see Step 2).
- A variety of craft materials (markers, pipe cleaners, Styrofoam® forms, colored construction paper, tape, glue, scissors, yarn, old magazines and catalogs, et cetera). Experiment with a diversity of craft materials for different sessions.
- A variety of magazines (optional).

Procedure

1. Form participants into groups of five to ten people and ask them to identify a problem. Have the group tell a negative story about how the problem manifests itself in their organization.

2. Have each group circle around four pieces of flipchart paper, with the following headings written on the top of the flipchart paper:

   "Once upon a time. . ." (introduce the characters and set the stage)

   "Then one day. . ." (a precipitating event occurs)

   "And so. . ." (what happens)

   "In the end. . ." (how it turns out)

   (These prompts create a storyboard to structure group stories. Use any other prompts you think might be helpful.)

3. Have them tell their stories as if they were fictional (thus, the language of "once upon a time"). Do not use names of the actual characters involved; instead, creatively rename the characters (for example, "The fire breathing dragon") and "color" the story by elaborating and embellishing it.

4. Advise the group that they can use the craft materials to help them tell their stories. Suggest they also consider using images from magazines as visual metaphors around which to build their stories.

5. Based on size of the group, specify an amount of time for them to complete the activity; 15 to 30 minutes typically is sufficient for five to eight people.

6. Visit each group to provide encouragement and help with any difficulties that might arise. As the groups begin to finish, tell them they will share their stories with the larger group. (This will allow them to prepare thoughtfully.)

7. Have each group present its storyboards and discuss its story with the larger audience. Remind them that they are telling a fictional story.

8. Ask other participants to engage in dialogue with the group doing the telling. Encourage them to clarify any questions and avoid any problem solving. They should keep focused on the story and suspend assumptions. For example, when talking about the story's action, refer to "When the main character. . ." as opposed to, "When Sally said. . ."

9. Once the groups have described their problems in a fictional manner (thus allowing themselves some distance from the problems), tell them they will be moving into a second phase, imaginative "restoryation," a

167

way for groups to "restory" their negative stories into more positive and healthy ones.

10. Have each group circle around four pieces of flipchart paper with the same headings used in Step 2.

11. Say that you want them to tell the story of a desired future—what they imagine the new, positive story to be. Again, encourage them not to use names of the "real" characters. Instead, have them creatively rename the characters (for example, "The heroine with wings") and elaborate and embellish the story.

12. Advise the group that they can again use the craft materials to help tell their stories. (Groups often will seek out new images and metaphors to describe the imagined future.)

13. Based on size of the group, specify an amount of time for them to complete the activity; 15 to 30 minutes typically is sufficient for five to eight people.

14. Visit each group to provide encouragement and help with any difficulties that might arise. As the groups begin to finish, remind them that they will share their stories with the larger group. (This will allow them to prepare thoughtfully.)

15. Have each group present its storyboards and discuss its story with the larger audience. Remind them that they are telling an imagined story of their desired future.

16. Ask other participants to engage in dialogue with the group doing the telling. Encourage them to clarify any questions and avoid any problem solving. They should keep focused on the story and suspend assumptions. For example, when talking about the story's action, refer to "When the main character. . ." versus "When Sally said. . . ." At this point each group will have given voice to their stories through imaginative "restoryation," thus "restorying" the formerly dominant, negative story lines.

Discussion

Say to the participants:

"Through fictionalization of an issue, this activity helps provide new problem perspectives. Once a problem is defined, imaginative 'restoryation' allows you to envision an imagined future or desired result by 're-storying.' This allows you to turn a dysfunctional and dominant organizational story line into a healthier story. The result is 'restoration' of more functional behaviors of a team or organization."

Lead a discussion with the participants, addressing differences between each group's fictionalizations and imaginative restoryations. Ask such questions as:

- What new possibilities were imagined?
- How were those possibilities realized?
- Who was responsible for those new possibilities and what were their characteristics?
- How did they bring about the changes?
- What obstacles did they have to overcome?
- What was the compelling vision that created positive movement in the new stories?

Then, shift attention away from the stories and try to connect to the "real" issue that the group is dealing with, asking questions such as:

- Can you see yourself in the imaginative restoryation?
- How could you act similarly to the characters in the imaginative restoryation?
- What visual images or metaphors could serve you as you seek to realize this new story line?
- How might you use what you learned from this exercise to improve team collaboration or performance?

Variation

If a group already has defined its problem clearly or if there is excessive "negative energy" around a problem, it can use just the imagined restoryation process (Steps 10 to 16).

Contributor

Nick Nissley is an assistant professor of organization learning and development at the University of St. Thomas in Minneapolis. Nissley teaches, writes, and consults on how arts-based learning (including storytelling) can be used as a means of making sense of organizations and organizational life.

IT'S HISTORY

Objectives

- To create positive team expectations
- To review and build on group accomplishments
- To help team members empower themselves as a group

Uses

- Strategic planning
- Team building
- Visioning

Art Form

Storytelling

Time Required

60 minutes

Materials, Handouts, and Equipment

- One flipchart for each group
- Two markers for each group
- Computer (optional)
- Computer projector (optional)
- Overhead projector (optional)

Procedure

1. Divide participants into small groups of four to five people each, ideally natural work units. (Members of larger groups can be subdivided and the results compared.)

2. Tell the groups to brainstorm a list of at least five group "stories" that in some way helped to define the team, for better or worse, for instance, the "Smith Project" when the team was able to pull together and meet a difficult deadline; the "Jones Incident" when one team member let down the others. They should record these stories on a flipchart or computer screen (if the group is small enough or a computer projector is available).

3. Instruct the groups to select one story that resonates best with the whole team and brainstorm major facts and opinions about the story. Have them record this information on a flipchart or computer.

4. When they have finished recording this information, ask them to rewrite this story, but this time with a different ending, so if the original story had a positive ending, they should write one with a negative ending and vice versa.

5. Have them discuss this new story and extract major learning outcomes they might use to enhance team performance and collaboration in the future.

6. Ask each group to share its old and new stories, plus what group members learned, with the large group.

Discussion

Use the following questions to help guide a discussion:

- Were any of the stories more myth than fact? (Both can be useful.)
- Based on your new stories, what might you do differently? Why?
- What might you repeat? Why?
- Can a story with a positive ending provide as much learning as one with a negative ending? Why?
- What common elements were there across all the stories? What differences were there?
- How might you create an organizational knowledge base of these and other stories? What resources would you need? How could you motivate people to contribute to it and use the stories?

Variation

Ask participants to think of stories prior to the activity, distribute them to other participants, and then obtain a vote on the favored stories to use.

Contributor

Arthur VanGundy, Ph.D., works as a creativity consultant, trainer, and facilitator of brainstorming retreats. He is the author of ten books, including *Techniques of Structured Problem Solving, Training Your Creative Mind, Managing Group Creativity, Brain Boosters for Business Advantage,* and *101 Great Games & Activities*. Major clients include Hershey Foods, S.C. Johnson Company, Xerox, Motorola, Sunbeam, Air Canada, Monsanto, Wyeth-Ayerst Pharmaceuticals, and the Singapore government. He also is founder of All Star Minds, a global Internet brainstorming service.

ONCE UPON A TEAM

Objectives

- To clarify core group values and norms
- To foster a spirit of teamwork and collaboration
- To practice creative thinking
- To improve communication spontaneity

Uses

- Values clarification
- Team building
- Leadership

Art Forms

- Storytelling
- Improvisation

Time Required

60 minutes

Materials, Handouts, and Equipment

- One copy of the Once Upon a Team handout for each participant
- One pen or pencil for each participant
- One flipchart for each group
- Two markers for each flipchart

Procedure

1. Distribute the Once Upon a Team handout and pens or pencils to members of small groups of four to seven people each.

2. Ask each group member to read the handout and fill in the blank spaces as indicated. They should not deliberate very long, but fill in the blanks as quickly as possible.

3. After everyone has finished, ask for volunteers to share their completed stories within their groups. If time is short, read at least three stories.

4. Tell the other group members to make notes about the team-related values represented by each story as it is read.

5. After all the stories have been read, tell the group members to review their notes.

6. Have each group analyze the values or norms represented in each story and record them on a flipchart. (Some stories may need to be repeated.) Examples of value and norm topics include trust, communication, leadership, power, freedom, fear, self-sufficiency, cooperation, competition, defensiveness, empowerment, and friendship.

7. Instruct the groups to review all the values listed, organize them into common clusters, and discuss any implications for team collaboration.

Discussion

Use the following questions to lead a discussion with all participants:

- How easy was it to think of answers to fill in the blanks? Why was it easy or difficult?
- Were the stories mostly serious or humorous? Why was that?
- What seemed to be the most frequently mentioned values?
- What values were not mentioned that you believe should have been?
- What did you learn about your group or individuals in it that you did not know before?
- What were the most significant implications for team collaboration?

Variations

1. Have the groups create their own stories with blanks for other groups to fill in.

2. Have members of each group fill in the blanks as an entire unit, rather than individually.

Contributor

Arthur VanGundy, Ph.D., works as a creativity consultant, trainer, and facilitator of brainstorming retreats. He is the author of ten books, including *Techniques of Structured Problem Solving, Training Your Creative Mind, Managing Group Creativity, Brain Boosters for Business Advantage,* and *101 Great Games & Activities*. Major clients include Hershey Foods, S.C. Johnson Company, Xerox, Motorola, Sunbeam, Air Canada, Monsanto, Wyeth-Ayerst Pharmaceuticals, and the Singapore government. He also is founder of All Star Minds, a global Internet brainstorming service.

Once Upon a Team

Complete the blanks in the following story:

"Once upon a time, there were _____ employees who worked in the
                                [number]

_____ for _____. Sometimes they
[department or work unit]   [company/organization]

were very happy when _____ happened; other times they were very
                         [event]

_____ when _____ happened. Some team members believed
[emotion]   [event]

that the team _____ very well during this times; others, however,
               [action verb]

thought that the _____ needed to improve its _____. The team
                  [noun]   [noun]

manager was a very _____ person who always seemed to _____
                    [adjective]   [verb]

the team whenever they _____ . One day, _____
                       [action verb, past tense]   [person or group]

decided to _____ the team that it must _____ its _____.
            [verb]   [action verb]   [noun]

Most team members _____ very _____ with this _____.
                  [were/were not]   [adjective]   [noun]

In fact, most reacted _____. However, the _____ seemed to
                       [adverb]   [noun]

change whenever _____ happened. It was then that the team
                  [event]

_____ it must work harder at _____.
 [verb]   [action verb]

And so they lived _____ ever after. The _____."
                  [action verb, past tense]   [noun]

Reproduced from *Orchestrating Collaboration at Work* by Arthur B. VanGundy & Linda Naiman with permission of the publisher. Copyright © 2005 by Arthur B. VanGundy & Linda Naiman.

STORIES OF CHANGE

Objectives

- To create awareness of how people are affected by change
- To help examine the assumptions and mental models underlying stories
- To stimulate organizational change using change stories within intact teams
- To enable teams to see how others react to common changes
- To create an environment of trust in teams and organizations

Uses

- Leadership and management
- Change management
- Team building
- As a catalyst to examine the meanings team members assign to different issues
- To apply organizational systems thinking principles during change and transition

Art Forms

- Storytelling
- Drawing

Time Required

1 to 2 hours

Materials, Handouts, and Equipment

- A piece of blank paper for each participant
- Pens, markers, and crayons
- A copy of the Stories of Change handout for each participant

Procedure

1. Begin by distributing a copy of the Stories of Change handout and pens, markers, and crayons to each participant and explain that the iceberg is used as a metaphor for story development.

2. Ask participants to individually draw a picture representing the changes, opportunities, and struggles they face in their teams. Tell them to use symbols, metaphors, and pictures, but not words.

3. Ask them to describe, individually, how their stories reveal the meaning of events in their work lives. For instance, "Stories connect us to the events that happen around us. When we 'dig deep,' we can understand the assumptions and mental models that have shaped our stories and evaluate their usefulness. This is particularly important during times of transition and change."

4. Ask participants to find partners and take turns telling their stories. To the storytellers, say: "Share the story behind your picture. Be expressive and describe characters, plot, scenes, feelings, and meanings. Talk about the meaning of the symbols involved."

    To the story listeners, say: "Ask five 'Why?' questions to get to the deeper meaning in the story. For instance, 'Why did someone say something they did? Why did someone do something? Why did they use the picture they did?' Your quest is to help the storytellers gently uncover the meanings in their stories (their meanings, not yours!)."

5. Post the pictures on a wall for all to see.

6. Ask participants to identify any patterns or common themes in the collective stories, working first in a dyad with their original partners, then by combining the dyads into small groups.

7. With the large group, examine both similarities and differences in the drawings and stories. Ask: "What did you see?" and "What insights or opportunities are there in understanding these patterns?" Encourage participants to see that their "stories" may be different from reality. Say: "They are our active creations, based on assumptions and mental models we hold. Once understood, this enables us to move on, adapt, and revise our stories if needed and experience real change." Encourage them to consider whether they want to revise their change story in any way. Explain how expressing concerns about change often helps us become "unstuck."

Discussion

The following questions can be used to help guide the discussion:

- What implications do your stories have for team collaboration?
- What might your team do differently now that you have created your stories?
- What might your team do differently after listening to the other stories?
- What might you do differently to enhance collaboration in your team?
- What assumptions were uncovered in any of the stories that seem to hold the keys for improving team performance?

Contributors

Michele Lewski is in private practice as an organization consultant. Frank Lewski is an organization consultant working for a large telecommunications company. Both specialize in helping leaders develop themselves and their organizations, particularly in times of change and transition. Mr. Lewski's specialties are leadership and team development, organization change, and diversity. Ms. Lewski works in similar areas and has clients ranging from large telecommunications companies and financial firms to the governor's office in the Commonwealth of Kentucky, the leadership of a world-wide church, and school districts.

Stories of Change

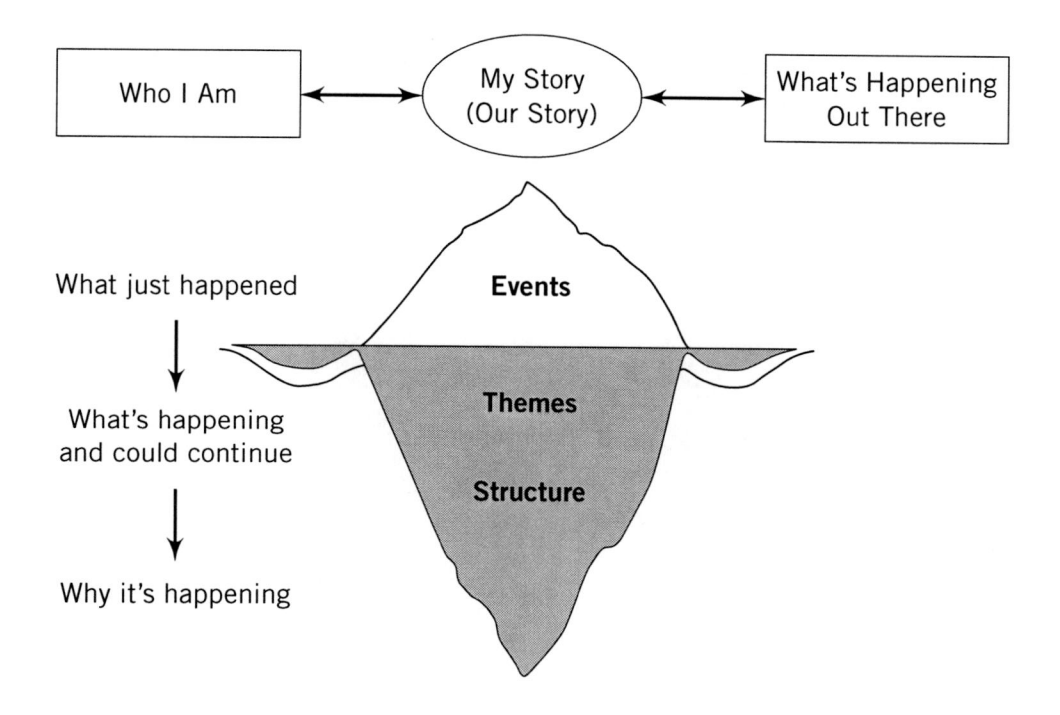

| Who I Am | ↔ | My Story (Our Story) | ↔ | What's Happening Out There |

What just happened
↓
What's happening and could continue
↓
Why it's happening

- Events
- Themes
- Structure

Reproduced from *Orchestrating Collaboration at Work* by Arthur B. VanGundy & Linda Naiman with permission of the publisher. Copyright © 2005 by Arthur B. VanGundy & Linda Naiman.

STORY LINES

Objectives

- To increase the ability to generate quantities of ideas
- To practice building on ideas of other team members
- To appreciate the value of free association in small groups
- To create a fun atmosphere within a group
- To brainstorm ways to improve group collaboration

Uses

- Creative thinking
- Warm-up
- Icebreaker
- Collaboration and cooperation

Art Forms

- Storytelling
- Improvisation

Time Required

10 to 15 minutes

Materials, Handouts, and Equipment

- One 8.5" x 11" piece of paper with "story lines" for each participant (see Step 1)
- One pen or pencil for each participant

Procedure

1. Prepare "story lines" for each participant. Print or write the opening of a hypothetical story at the top of a sheet of paper. Each participant should receive a different opening line. Samples include:
    - It was a dark and stormy night.
    - The sun blinded me as I walked out the door.

- You never know where a wrong turn will lead you.
- There is nothing greater than pure joy.
- The forest before me was dark and scary.
- I knew I should have gone back to the house.
- It was the last phone call I would ever receive.
- The dog looked hungry.
- "Follow me!" he said, as he bravely jumped out of the car.
- The heart is a lonely punter.
- 'Twas the night before Melvin.
- I never promised you a garden hose.
- The camera finally told a lie.
- Sometimes it's better just to give in.
- The setting sun struggled to escape the inevitable void.
- When you're right, you're right (sometimes).
- Head spinning, Ralph fell into the vat of oozing, red jam.
- I had no idea that I actually would have to dance.
- She had a beautiful smile, but there was something sinister about it.
- "Do you want the last piece of pizza?" Gerald mumbled.
- The night suddenly slithered away into the new light.

2. Organize participants into small groups of four to seven people. (Ideally, these would be natural work units.)

3. Distribute the paper and pens or pencils to each participant.

4. Instruct the participants to read the story line on their paper and write the next sentence that seems to flow from the first. Tell them to "free associate" this sentence and not think too long about what to write.

5. After everyone has written one sentence, tell them to pass their papers to the person on their right.

6. Once they receive the paper from their left, have them read the two sentences and add a third that would seem to follow from the two preceding sentences. Continue this process until everyone's original paper has circulated twice around the group. (For instance, in a five-person group, each story would be ten lines long.)

7. Ask each person to read the story on their paper and then have the group use this story to brainstorm ways to improve group collaboration, either within a work unit or between work teams.

8. Instruct each group to select the best two ideas and share with the larger group.

Discussion

Use the following questions to help guide a discussion:

- How easy was it to think of the next sentence from the preceding one? Why was it easy or difficult?

- Did you find yourself judging your initial response? If so, would you respond more freely now? Why or why not?

- One purpose of this exercise was to demonstrate how difficult it is to keep an open mind, even with a seemingly irrelevant task. What did you learn from this exercise that you could apply to collaboration or performance within your work group?

- How would you evaluate the quantity and quality of the ideas you generated? Do you think you could have produced the same quantity and quality without having done this exercise (that is, without using the stories)?

- How might you modify this exercise for other team uses such as improving communication?

Contributor

Arthur VanGundy, Ph.D., president of VanGundy & Associates, works as a creativity consultant, trainer, and facilitator of brainstorming retreats. He is the author of ten books, including *Techniques of Structured Problem Solving, Training Your Creative Mind, Managing Group Creativity, Brain Boosters for Business Advantage,* and *101 Great Games & Activities.* Major clients include Hershey Foods, S.C. Johnson Company, Xerox, Motorola, Sunbeam, Air Canada, Monsanto, Wyeth-Ayerst Pharmaceuticals, and the Singapore government. He also is founder of All Star Minds, a global Internet brainstorming service.

STORY WEAVING

Objectives

- To create a common understanding of a team's or organization's history
- To demonstrate the diverse perspectives of team or organization history and reactions to change

Uses

- Leadership
- Team development
- Understanding or closing the life of a team or organization
- Setting the stage for team or organizational change

Art Form

Storytelling

Time Required

90 minutes for five to fifteen participants

Materials, Handouts, and Equipment

- Large sheets of flipchart paper posted right next to each other across a long wall (at least 15 to 20 feet)
- Pens, markers, and crayons
- String or yarn
- Thumb tacks, push pins, or cellophane tape

Procedure

1. Prior to the session, post the paper on the wall and draw a horizontal timeline across the wallpaper, leaving equal space above and below.

2. Use vertical lines and divide the timeline into meaningful time periods in the life of the team or organization. Label the space above the line "Organization Events" (or "Team Events"), then label the space below "Individual Events, Reactions, and Feelings."

3. At the beginning of the session, point out the wallpaper and its labels to the participants.

4. Tell participants that they should be listing meaningful events above the timeline. They may depict changes, key milestones, successes, failures, or any other meaningful events. Below the line, they should list their personal corresponding feelings, reactions, milestones, "high points," "low points," or anything else meaningful to them regarding the events.

5. Have participants, collectively, approach the timeline and begin "charting." Encourage them to use symbols, metaphors, and pictures written (words also may be used) at various points on the timeline to illustrate the events and their feelings about them.

6. Invite participants to attach a string to connect each of their individual submissions (below the line) using tacks or tape. This enables viewers to "see the thread" of each participant as it is "woven" through the story.

7. Conduct a "read-out" for each time period. Have each person tell the story of what he or she charted in that time period. Ask participants to describe what they saw as meaningful events, their own reactions, and what they were feeling and experiencing at the time.

Discussion

Guide a post-exercise discussion using the following questions:

- What stories do the timelines tell?
- What patterns or common themes exist in the collective stories relevant to team collaboration?
- What does your story say about your team or organization?
- What can be learned from these histories?
- What did you notice about individuals' reactions?
- How much diversity was there in their reactions?
- How might events in this exercise affect team collaboration or performance?

Whenever possible, make connections between this discussion and team or organizational issues (for example, celebration, moving forward, or achieving closure).

Contributors

Michele Lewski is in private practice as an organization consultant. Frank Lewski is an organization consultant working for a large telecommunications company. Both specialize in helping leaders develop themselves and their organizations, particularly in times of change and transition. Mr. Lewski's specialties are leadership and team development, organization change, and diversity. Ms. Lewski works in similar areas and has clients ranging from large telecommunications companies and financial firms to the governor's office in the Commonwealth of Kentucky, the leadership of a world-wide church, and school districts.

TIME CAPSULE

Objectives

- To help preserve team and organizational cultures
- To improve team decision making
- To increase awareness of team values

Uses

- Communication
- Decision making

Art Form

Storytelling

Time Required

1 to 2 hours

Materials, Handouts, and Equipment

- A container to hold miscellaneous artifacts and collectibles for each sub-group
- Artifacts and collectibles representative of a work team or organization (for example, business cards, videos, posters, annual reports, invitations, mascots, photos marking special events, magazines, newspaper headlines) brought by participants (see Step 1)

Procedure

1. Before the session, instruct the participants to gather artifacts and collectibles of the team or organization that best represent its culture and significant events over a predetermined time. Tell them to bring these items to the session.

2. Begin the session by saying the following aloud to all participants:

    "A time capsule is defined in *The Oxford English Dictionary* (1989) as, 'a container used to store for posterity a selection of objects thought to be representative of life at a particular time.' A time capsule can be viewed as a form of conceptual art, creating an artifact that represents our culture and history-making moments. In creating a time capsule, we must assess the value of each item, each choice, each viewpoint, and then choose the most salient items."

3. As a large group, discuss the merits of a time capsule. Ask: "What would you like to include in your team's time capsule?" "What do these choices symbolize?"

4. Divide the participants into small groups, preferably natural work units.

5. Ask the groups to select from among the items brought by participants what will be included in their time capsules and to think about suitable containers. Suggest that they include a mix of items from the sublime to the trivial.

6. Have the groups decide on a retrieval date. (One consulting firm recently opened up their twenty-five-year archive box and took great delight in the nostalgia it stirred up. They also had a visible reminder of how much they had grown and evolved over the last quarter century.) Ask the participants how people might respond to their time capsule one hundred years from now.

7. Tell the groups to use the items in their time capsules to develop a story about the history of their team. Ask them, "What events were defining moments in the history of your team?"

8. Have each group choose an "archivist" or director to coordinate the project and find a secure location for storage. The archivist should keep an inventory of all items sealed in the time capsule.

9. Explain that the International Time Capsule Society (ITCS) offers the following advice:

    - Find a secure indoor location. It is not recommended that time capsules be "buried." Thousands have been lost this way. It is important that the location be marked with a plaque describing the "mission" of the time capsule.

    - Have a solemn "sealing ceremony" where you formally name the time capsule. Invite the media and keep a photographic record of your efforts, including the inside of your completed project.

    - Don't forget your time capsule! You would be surprised how often this happens, usually within a short time. Try to "renew" the tradition of memory with anniversaries and reunions. You also might send out invitations to the projected opening. Use your creativity at all times.

Discussion

Use the following questions to help guide a discussion:

- What thoughts and feelings emerged from this exercise?
- How easy or difficult was it to make choices?
- What does the time capsule symbolize to you?
- What aspects of team culture came to light during this session?
- What would you like to celebrate about your team's culture?
- What is missing from your team's culture?
- What narrative emerged from the construction of this time capsule?
- How might this experience enhance your team performance?

Contributor

Linda Naiman, BFA, works with organizations to awaken genius-level thinking through the art and science of applying creativity, innovation, and visionary thinking to business strategy. Naiman is a life-long artist and presents workshops on creativity and innovation in North America and Europe.

TO GO WHERE NO GROUP HAS GONE BEFORE

Objectives

- To use metaphor to explore individual strengths of team members
- To create a group vision for collaboration
- To create awareness about hidden, individual strengths
- To understand that job titles reveal only a piece of what team members can offer
- To learn the importance of first understanding points of view, disclosing, and then integrating individual strengths (rather than attempting first to arrive at a consensus about a group vision)

Uses

- Leadership
- Team building
- Self-exploration
- Skill building
- Listening
- Communication

Art Form

Storytelling

Time Required

90 minutes

Materials, Handouts, and Equipment

- One copy of the Darmok and Jalad at Tenagra sheet for the facilitator
- At least fifty name tags with metaphorical phrases (the number will vary with group size) to provide choice among participants. There should be at least three copies of each tag. Suggestions for name tags include:
    - I Am the Bear that Walks Backwards
    - I Am the Sun that Never Sets

- I Am a River that Flows
- I Am a Quiet Storm
- I Sing with Birds
- I Run with the Pack
- I Run as Swiftly as a Gazelle
- I Howl with the Wind
- I Am the Strength of Mountains
- I Am the Eagle that Sees
- I Am the Alert Creature, Up at Dawn
- I Am the Gate to an Inner Courtyard
- I Am the Glimmering Lights of the City
- One table for spreading art materials (including name tags)
- One table for each group to sit, write, and process together
- One of the following for each participant:
  - Pen
  - Marker
  - Paper for timed writing
  - Magazine picture cutouts (optional for variation)
  - Glue sticks (optional for variation)

Procedure

1. Have the participants form into small groups of four to seven and take turns introducing themselves by name, department, role they play within that department or organization, and the number of years employed there.

2. Invite a discussion of the assumptions about those roles that team members may make. Ask them to consider how such assumptions might prevent a group from reaching more creative applications and solutions.

3. Read the Star Trek "Darmok and Jalad at Tenagra" story and tell the participants just to listen.

4. Introduce the concept of metaphor. Note how it typically is a figure of speech used to make a comparison—for example, saying that someone is a snake.

5. Invite the participants to choose from the art table a name tag that resonates with them, as well as writing materials.

6. Instruct them to elaborate and write for 10 to 12 minutes on the metaphor represented by the name tag they chose.

7. Invite the participants to share their writing within their groups.

8. Have the participants return to the larger group for sharing. Ask for ways these metaphors—or the process of writing about the name tag they chose—might apply to their teams and to their work.

Discussion

Lead a discussion using the following questions:

- What did it feel like to do this metaphor exercise (from choosing the name tag, to writing about it, to sharing it with your small group)?

- Were there any assumptions you made during the first round of introductions from your team members? Were those assumptions different from or similar to any you noticed when team members shared their metaphors?

- What did you learn about team members? Were there any surprises?

- Can you think of some ways to apply this metaphor writing process to collaborating on a team project?

- How might this process help you to be more effective as team members? As leaders? As visionaries? As communicators? In resolving conflict?

Variations

1. Ask people to create a collage using additional art materials as well as phrases from poems. Spread the collages around the perimeter of the table and have people do a silent walk around to witness the individual metaphor collages of their team. Complete Step 8 of the process.

2. Ask the group to brainstorm areas in which they want to create breakthroughs (for example, communication, listening, accountability, time management). Write these on a blackboard or flipchart. Depending on the size of the group and the number of ideas generated, create teams of no fewer than four to work on each suggested breakthrough. Divide the participants into groups so that some will be working on communication, others on time management, et cetera.

3. Have participants use the same metaphor exercise, but generate their own vision statements of who they are relative to those topics. Tell them that the task is to come up with a group vision of who they are as a team, relative to the breakthrough. When they are done, have them share any breakthroughs and insights.

Contributors

John Fox, certified poetry therapist, is an associate professor at the California Institute for Integral Studies and an adjunct professor at the Institute for Transpersonal Psychology and the John F. Kennedy University Graduate School of Holistic Studies.

Lisa DeVuono is a creativity coach.

Darmok and Jelad at Tenagra

There is a famous episode of "Star Trek: The Next Generation," called Darmok, where Captain Jean Luc Picard is beamed down to a planet with a Tamarian named Dathon. Dathon also is a captain and, like Picard, is a leader of accomplishment and intelligence. Their mutual goal is to develop bridges of understanding, but communication between the two is virtually impossible. Picard's thinking and speech are straightforward and rational. Dathon, on the other hand, can only think and speak in poetic terms. When Dathon sees their campfire about to go out, he says something like, "Our stars are fading away." Picard is unable to recognize the link between the embers of the campfire and the stars. When Picard also notices the fire dying out and insists they gather wood, Dathon does not have a clue what Picard means, because he is unable to link his inner poetic experience with practical action.

This story illustrates the split between the rational, logical mind and the creative, poetic soul. Picard tried to proceed logically in solving their dilem-ma, but this led only to further exasperation. Dathon, on the other hand, became more lonely and withdrawn. Unable to convey all he experienced and felt, he became depressed. Picard began to listen and saw the value of Dathon's poetic communication and Dathon saw a way to put his inner world into action. Through this process of recognition and connection both were able to decipher the other's language and reduce their communication breakdown.

This linking of seemingly different entities is the special, liberating role of metaphor. The making of metaphor opens a window where the inner and outer aspects of our lives can join. Poetic devices such as metaphor, simile, voice, and image allow us to make what is perceived within the heart come to light in our writing. Metaphors can give us a wholly new perspective; but they are not especially mysterious. Like Picard learning to communicate with Dathon, you can learn to make them too.

Reproduced from *Orchestrating Collaboration at Work* by Arthur B. VanGundy & Linda Naiman with permission of the publisher. Copyright © 2005 by Arthur B. VanGundy & Linda Naiman.

11 Theater Improvisation

- The Advocates
- The Answer Is Always Yes
- Ball Toss Chaos
- Free Association Word Ball
- Obstacles and Opportunities
- Reflections
- Statues
- Team Moving
- Two Minutes of Fame
- The World's Worst Leader

THE ADVOCATES

Objectives

- To teach people how to act as an advocate for new ideas
- To help people articulate difficult positions
- To improve interpersonal debating skills
- To develop creative thinking skills

Uses

- Conflict management
- Interpersonal persuasion
- Selling new ideas

Art Form

Improvisational theater

Time Required

Approximately 30 to 45 minutes (2 minutes per advocate, 1 minute for comments from each board member)

Materials, Handouts, and Equipment

- A list of positions for advocacy based on the topic area of the meeting, training, or session (see the Sample Topic Areas list for examples)

Procedure

1. Prior to the session, determine the subject matter (inventions, research, unusual political parties, and so forth) and create the advocacy topics. The subject matter is not important, but the topics should be as outrageous as possible.

2. Introduce The Advocates as a special occasion in which a group of "experts" has gathered to advocate the value of their unique positions to a board of directors.

3. Divide the participants into two groups—Advocates and Board of Directors.

4. One by one, invite an "expert" to the front of the room and show that advocate the position he or she will be expected to advocate.

5. Give the advocate 2 minutes to persuade the Board of Directors of the value of his or her unique position.

6. Continue the procedure until all the experts have advocated an idea.

7. Have each member of the board take 1 minute to comment on the worthiness/weakness of each advocate's argument.

8. Tell them to switch roles and repeat with a new topic.

Discussion

Some sample debriefing questions include:

- What was your first reaction when you saw your advocacy position?
- Did you think you could be an effective advocate for that topic?
- What techniques did you use to advocate your position?
- Did those techniques work?
- What did you observe when watching others advocate their positions?
- What conclusions can you draw from this activity?

Be sure that participants realize that anyone can advocate for any subject if required to do so.

Contributor

Lenn Millbower is the author of *Training with a Beat, Cartoons for Trainers, Show Biz Training,* and *Game Show Themes for Trainers.* He is a magician, a music arranger, a pianist, an instructional designer, and an educator who combines entertainment and learning into interventions that are creative, meaningful, and fun.

Sample Topic Areas

Sample One

An automotive company seeking a breakthrough idea for enhancing their cars.

The ideas to be advocated:

- Alien Abduction Kit
- Concrete Bumpers
- Driver's Seat Hammocks
- Edible Upholstery
- New Car Smell Spray
- Oblong Wheels
- Retractable Road Maps
- Seven Wheel Cars

Sample Two

A sporting goods store seeking new products to sell.
The ideas to be advocated:

- Bottled Locker Room Scent
- Combination Boxing/Baseball Glove
- Disposable Basketballs
- Edible Hockey Pucks
- Halloween Hockey Masks
- Raw Egg Baseballs
- See-Through Jerseys
- Wooden Tennis Shoes

Reproduced from *Orchestrating Collaboration at Work* by Arthur B. VanGundy & Linda Naiman with permission of the publisher. Copyright © 2005 by Arthur B. VanGundy & Linda Naiman.

THE ANSWER IS ALWAYS YES

Objectives

- To exercise the imagination
- To encourage participants to look beyond the initial knee-jerk response to a question
- To foster spontaneous creative responses under pressure

Uses

- A warm-up for brainstorming sessions
- Practice for interview situations

Art Form

Improvisational theater

Time Required

20 to 30 minutes

Procedure

1. Ask the participants to form pairs. One is to play the role of interviewer and one to play the role of interviewee.

2. Instruct the interviewers to ask the interviewees "yes" or "no" questions that would be difficult to respond to with a "yes." For example: "Is it true that you are the offspring of Elvis Presley and a space alien?"

3. Note that participants should avoid asking questions that might offend the interviewees. Share some positive—although still preposterous—questions when introducing the exercise, such as: "Is it true that you are planning to run for president?" or "Did you win the lottery last month?"

4. Tell the interviewees that they must say "yes" to each question, wholeheartedly embracing that which is hard to accept. The interviewee then must add some additional information about the situation. For instance, consider the question: "Is it true that you are the offspring of Elvis Presley and a space alien?" One answer might be: "Yes, and I'd love to take you all for a ride on my blue suede spaceship." Another possibility: "Yes, and you'd be amazed at how the people on mom's home planet respond when I sing there."

5. After each questioner has asked the interviewee one question, have the participants switch roles so the interviewer becomes the interviewee and vice versa.

6. After pairs have completed their interviews, ask them to switch partners with another pair and conduct the interviews again.

Discussion

Use the following questions to help guide a discussion:

- Did you find it easier to be the interviewee or the questioner?
- What did you discover when asked questions to which you found it difficult to say "yes"?
- How easy was it for you to divorce yourself from more familiar realities and invent new ones?
- How frequently do you have to improvise communication within your work team?
- Do you think there is a relationship between the ability of team members to think on their feet and team effectiveness?
- In what situations might the ability to improvise statements in teams be dysfunctional?

Contributor

Jacquie Lowell, M.Ed., has been leading creativity and improvisational comedy workshops for twenty-five years. Drawing on experience in theater, dance, psychology, and metaphysics, she has developed lively creativity-stimulating exercises and training programs for companies, organizations, conferences, and schools. She also directs the Creative Urges and Mission Improvible improvisational comedy troupes.

BALL TOSS CHAOS

Objectives

- To help a group become aware of their reactions to unanticipated change
- To illustrate how we can develop new strategies and patterns "on the fly" when confronted with new challenges
- To enhance the ability of teams to focus on a task

Uses

- Energizer
- Team building
- Change management
- Creative, flexible thinking

Art Form

Improvisational theater

Time Required

20 to 30 minutes

Materials, Handouts, and Equipment

- Three balls or something else that can be tossed (large earmuffs that fold into a ball are best, since they don't bounce away when dropped)

Procedure

1. Have participants form two lines facing each other. For example, line one could be made up of Chloe, Laura, and Sarah. Facing them in line two are Ralph, Ben, and Don, respectively. Chloe is directly across from Ralph, Laura across from Ben, and Sarah across from Don.

2. Give the participant at the end of one line a ball and tell him or her to toss it to the person directly across from them.

3. Have the first person toss the ball to the person in the other line directly across from him or her. Thus, Don would toss the ball to Sarah, who is directly across from him.

4. Instruct the person who receives the ball to throw it to the person in the other line who is standing next to the person who threw the ball originally. Thus, because Don threw the ball to Sarah, she would throw it to the person standing next to Don, Ben. Ben then would toss the ball to the person directly across from him, who is Laura (standing next to Sarah). Laura, in turn, would throw the ball to the person standing next to Ben, who is Ralph. (See illustration.)

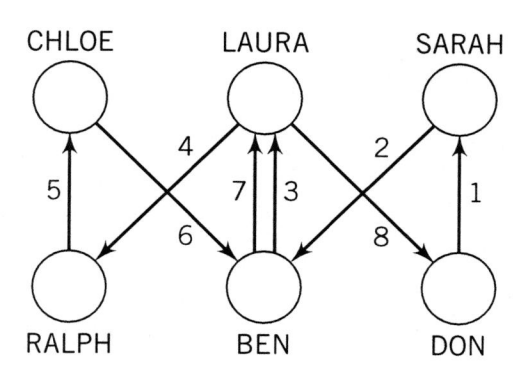

```
CHLOE        LAURA        SARAH
  ○            ○            ○
      4            2
  5       7  3          1
      6            8
  ○            ○            ○
RALPH         BEN          DON
```

5. Have everyone repeat this zigzag pattern down the line until the last person to receive a ball receives it.

6. Tell the last person to receive the ball and send it back, passing it to the person standing next to the person who threw it to him or her, and to maintain this pattern throughout the activity. In the example above, if Chloe was the last person to receive the ball she would throw it to Ben, as he is standing next to Ralph, the person who originally tossed the ball to her. Ben then would throw the ball to Laura, since she is standing next to Chloe.

7. Continue by repeating Steps 3 through 6, but provide the following directions for variation (in improv parlance, "side coaching"):

  • Silent toss: Toss the ball without speaking.

  • Call your name: The tosser says his or her name when tossing the ball.

  • Call recipient's name: The tosser says the recipient's name when tossing the ball.

  • Speak or sing the "Row, Row, Row" song lyrics, one word at a time, with each tosser calling out the next word in the song when he or she tosses the ball: "Row, row, row your boat/Gently down the stream/Merrily, merrily, merrily, merrily/Life is but a dream."

8. After a few minutes, tell the participants to stop singing and to continue tossing the ball silently as instructed originally.

9. After a couple of minutes, tell the participant at the end of one line that, when the ball reaches the other end of the line, that participant should start singing the first word of the "Row, Row, Row" song and send it back down the line, one word at a time.

10. Tell the group to change direction of the ball toss when you raise your right hand and that they should continue singing throughout the rest of the steps.

11. Tell the group to change direction of the ball toss when you raise your left hand.

12. Start a second ball down the line, using the same pattern of the first ball and the singing.

13. Start a third ball down the line using the same pattern of the previous balls and the singing.

14. Encourage the participants to keep the game going, even if they make a mistake or "freeze" when the song gets to them. They should try to recover as quickly as possible. Saying anything or even just passing is preferred to stammering or apologizing for making a mistake.

Discussion

Conclude the activity with a discussion based on the following questions:

- How is this game like "real life" work teams? Possible answers:
  - You've got many balls in the air at once.
  - The rules change in midstream.
  - There is a lot coming at you all at once, from many directions.
  - There is a lot of room for error.
- What's required in order to be successful in teams that you learned from this activity? Possible answers:
  - You must react quickly under pressure.
  - You need to be able to track multiple things at once.
  - You need to try to get into the flow of the activity and trust your intuition.
  - We need to become aware that we have the capacity to adapt quickly to change by developing new patterns that will help us with the current reality.

- Sometimes you don't feel like you're doing "perfectly" or have all the information needed to proceed, but proceeding anyway is preferable to being paralyzed (likely nobody else will notice your lack of "perfection").
- What could your team borrow from this exercise to improve team leadership? Team decision making?
- If some members had difficulty following the directions, how did the others react? What might they have done differently if their reaction was negative?

Variations

1. Tell the participants to create a "word-at-a-time" story about the training topic when they toss the ball.
2. Incorporate music, sound effects, and percussion.
3. Relax the rules if the participants seem to have trouble following directions.

Contributor

Jerry Kail is an internal organization development and training consultant specializing in change management, innovation, human performance development, team development, and group facilitation. He also performs with the Dayton-based improv troupe, Strangely Attractive, and is a passionate explorer of improv and other theater-based applications to the organizational world.

FREE ASSOCIATION WORD BALL

Objectives

- To promote quick thinking and mental fluency and flexibility
- To energize participants who have been sitting for a long time

Uses

- Warm-up
- An energizer during a meeting or sedentary session
- Verbal and nonverbal communication within groups

Art Form

Theater improvisation

Time Required

5 to 10 minutes

Materials, Handouts, and Equipment

- One easy-to-catch, small rubber or foam ball for each group of six to eight participants

Procedure

1. Have groups of six to eight participants form standing circles in a roomy area.

2. Give a ball to player "1" in each group. Tell player 1 to makes eye contact with another person in the group, say any word aloud, and toss the ball to that person. The recipient then makes eye contact with someone else in the group, says whatever word player 1's word brought to mind, and tosses the ball to the next recipient.

3. Continue this cycle until everyone in the circle has had several chances to free-associate with a previous player's word.

4. Remind participants to let go of all prior thoughts and free-associate only with the word said by the person who throws the ball to them.

Discussion

Discussion questions for participants:

- How difficult was it to let go of earlier associations and respond only to the person who threw the ball to you?
- Did you have trouble hanging onto an association from the previous player? Why or why not?
- What did you notice about other people's associations? About your own?
- How can the ability to spontaneously free associate affect team performance? Affect team collaboration?
- How important was nonverbal communication during this exercise? Why?

Contributor

Jacquie Lowell, M.Ed., has been leading creativity and improvisational comedy workshops for twenty-five years. Drawing on experience in theater, dance, psychology, and metaphysics, she has developed lively creativity-stimulating exercises and training programs for companies, organizations, conferences, and schools. She also directs The Creative Urges and Mission Improvible improvisational comedy troupes.

OBSTACLES AND OPPORTUNITIES

Objectives

- To increase group energy and focus
- To discover possibilities for new perspectives on current challenges
- To develop a kinesthetic awareness of different approaches to achieving goals

Uses

- Leadership
- Team building
- Warm-up
- Energizer

Art Form

Theater improvisation

Time Required

About 60 minutes

Materials, Handouts, and Equipment

- A bell or chime to delineate changes in directing the group's movement.
- A copy of the Reflection and Application Worksheet for each participant (optional)
- A very large meeting room or ballroom. The room should be large enough for participants to move freely throughout the area. Ideally, chairs and other furniture can be moved to the outer edges of the room to maximize available space. If space is limited, divide the group in half. While the first group participates, the others observe and vice versa. (Of course, this method will double the required time.)

Procedure

1. State the objectives of the activity and ask participants to stand and disperse themselves around the room so there is ample space between them.

2. Invite them to begin walking silently through the space at a comfortable, moderate pace.

3. Once participants begin walking through the space, direct their movement with various instructions such as:

"Now walk as if you are in a hurry."

"Walk as if you feel peaceful and contemplative."

"Walk as if you sense danger or tension."

"Move as if you are purposeful and determined."

It is helpful, although not necessary, to invite them to return to a moderate pace in between the above variations. The chime can be used as a signal to shift.

4. After returning to a moderate pace, invite the participants to each choose a direction and silently move as far as they can in that direction, until they are forced to change course to avoid an obstacle (for example, another person, a wall, furniture). Each time they change course, they should continue moving as far as they can in that direction until they must choose yet another direction. (The size of the space should be such that people can take at least four or five steps before they have to turn.) Allow the group to move in this manner for at least 1 minute.

5. While they are still moving as directed above, say to them: "Now, rather than moving in a straight line until you must adjust, begin to look for the open areas and move through the room by stepping into the open spaces. Continue to navigate through the space by always moving toward the open space." Allow the group to move in this new manner for at least 1 minute.

6. Ask them to notice how this feels different from the previous instruction. Then ring the chime and invite them to stop.

Discussion

Invite participants to share various reflections, first in pairs or trios and then with the whole group. If you wish, distribute copies of the Reflection and Application Worksheet and have people begin by writing their responses.

Questions that can guide the verbal reflection and application include:

- In general, what did you notice?
- How is it useful?

- What metaphors from nature come to mind in relation to this experience?
- What implications are there for team collaboration?
- How often does your work team stray from functional collaboration?
- In what circumstances does it seem useful to choose a course and stick to it?
- How might this exercise affect the way you walk through an airport, drive a car, or engage in other activities involving movement?
- Was your walking pace at the end of the exercise different than at the beginning? How? Why do you think this was so?
- In your current team:
  - Where are you running into obstacles? How might those shift?
  - Where are the open spaces? Opportunities?
  - Where could you use more direction, support, clarity, or resources?
  - What direction could you offer for a current project/team/organization?
  - In what ways might our work environments affect how we navigate through them?

Variations

1. To assist in creating a safe environment for exploration and risk taking when offering experiential exercises, you might want to preface the exercise with the following guidelines. Although they seem somewhat paradoxical, they often are useful. Remind participants that they possess free will and all participation is voluntary. Thus, they can choose to witness any exercise the group will explore. Then remind them you are intentionally choosing activities that will bring a fresh perspective and create new avenues of learning that may, by their very nature, seem unfamiliar or unusual. Ask participants to notice if an activity feels uncomfortable. Encourage them to be willing to acknowledge their discomfort and to stretch themselves—to expand beyond that limitation—by exploring *with* the group.

To demonstrate the above, you might invite people to sit or stand comfortably. Then have them gently raise their arms up over their heads and notice how it feels. Then invite them to raise their arms as high as they can, stretching toward the ceiling, and notice how that feels different. For some, the stretching sensation may feel pleasurable; for others it may feel less comfortable than with arms merely raised or with arms at their sides. In general, it is unlikely anyone will report that it is actually painful. Discuss this distinction between sensation and pain, noting again that part of experiential work may generate sensations that may be perceived as "out of one's comfort zone." However, it is not intended or likely to create pain. With the above distinction in mind, once again invite the group to explore the exercises and their responses to them with curiosity, that is, to be willing to stretch.

2. Once participants are walking through the space, you can subdivide the group with a variety of random criteria. For example: If some people are wearing blue, have them walk as if in a hurry. Or, if they crossed a bridge to attend the session, have them walk in slow motion.

3. Early on in the exercise, you can play with a wide variety of sensory and situational directions when inviting participants to walk through the space. For example: "Walk as if it is extremely hot/cold/windy/dark . . . as if wading through molasses . . . as if you are over budget and behind schedule . . . as if you are wildly successful."

Contributor

Nan Crawford & Co. provides experiential training and presentations. Crawford's work ignites creativity, confidence, and clarity—catalyzing breakthroughs in leadership, communication, collaboration, and performance. She holds an MA in organization development and is the artistic director of Pacific Playback Theatre. Clients include *Fast Company*, IBM, Lucent, More Than Money, Target, and Office Depot.

Reflection and Application Worksheet

This page is for your benefit and you will not be asked to show it to anyone else. Give yourself license to express your experience in individual words or phrases that come up as you reflect on how the exercise felt. Keep a constant flow of unedited writing for 2 minutes. Allow your hand to keep moving across the page. If needed, feel free to repeat words so that you can keep writing a steady stream of ideas, images, awareness, or insight.

1. Stream of consciousness writing in response to the movement exercise (2 minutes)

2. Where are you running into obstacles? What challenges do you face? How might those shift?

3. Where are the open spaces? Opportunities? What resources do you currently have?

4. What would generate increased openings, for example, allies, clarity, direction, additional resources, support, and so forth?

5. What are some next steps you can take to move into the open avenues? What direction could you offer for your current project, team, or organization?

Reproduced from Orchestrating Collaboration at Work by Arthur B. VanGundy & Linda Naiman with permission of the publisher. Copyright © 2005 by Arthur B. VanGundy & Linda Naiman.

6. Play with all of the words you have written in response to the questions above and the stream of consciousness section to create a haiku or short poem. A haiku is a three-line poem: five syllables for the first, seven for the second, and then five for the last.
    Ideas crystallized.

Reproduced from Orchestrating Collaboration at Work by Arthur B. VanGundy & Linda Naiman with permission of the publisher. Copyright © 2005 by Arthur B. VanGundy & Linda Naiman.

REFLECTIONS

Objectives

- To improve interpersonal communication skills
- To increase awareness of nonverbal communication
- To break down personality barriers

Uses

- Warm-up
- Energizer

Art Forms

- Mime
- Theater improvisation

Time Required

Approximately 15 minutes

Materials, Handouts, and Equipment

- Soft classical or light jazz background music (be sure to check copyright restrictions)
- A tape or CD player
- Video camera (optional) to track participants' progress over time

Procedure

1. Instruct participants to pair up. (If there is an odd number of people, the leader may participate.)
2. Explain that this exercise is intended to enhance communication and the exchange of information. However, participants must remain silent during the activity.
3. Select very soft, slow classical or light jazz as background music.
4. Have the pairs spread out in the room as far from others as possible.

5. Explain that inhibitions are common at the outset of this activity. However, with time, it becomes more familiar and comfortable.

6. Have each pair designate a leader and a follower and tell them they are to respond to each other as mirror images.

7. Instruct the leaders to make subtle hand and body motions while the followers try to copy or mimic these motions as a mirror image. The goal is to move in tandem.

8. After 2 to 3 minutes, have the pairs switch roles.

9. After another 2 to 3 minutes, tell the participants there are no leaders or followers. Their roles now are equal. They must take their cues from each other in a give-and-take manner. For instance, when one moves, the other reflects and then creates a new move for the other. However, neither person may assume a dominant role. The goal is to anticipate and read their partners' moves.

10. Reconvene the entire group and lead a group discussion.

Discussion

Use the following questions to help guide the discussion:

- How awkward was it to look at your partner so intently? Why was this true?
- Did this discomfort lessen as the activity continued? Why or why not?
- How easy was it to anticipate the leader's action when you were the follower?
- When you were the leader, how easy was it to convey your motions successfully to your partner so that the motions were carried out?
- When both participants had equal roles, were you more aware of the exchange of communication of motion? Why or why not?
- Do you feel you were better able to communicate with your partner at the end of the activity than at the beginning? Why was this?
- Was there any energy that passed between the two of you? If so, how would you describe it?
- What surprised you the most during this activity?
- What did you learn about your partner?

- What implications are there for team collaboration?
- How important is nonverbal communication for team collaboration? Why? Can you think of any examples?
- What did you learn about yourself?

Contributor

Janice Kilgore has varied experiences in the professional music world as well as being a devout music educator and musician. She was trained at the University of North Texas with degrees in music education (B.M., M.M.E.). She is currently working on a doctorate at UNT in creative thinking through music education applications. She has served as a consultant and lecturer since 1987 and is in over ten editions of *Who's Who,* including *Who's Who in Entertainment.* Ms. Kilgore has created a distance learning music education program for children and contributed several exercises in *101 Great Games and Activities.* She is currently on staff at Tarrant County College, Southeast Campus, as a music instructor.

STATUES

Objectives

- To discover roles and patterns in teams
- To explore alternative ways of working together

Uses

- Communication
- Team building
- Conflict resolution
- Leadership

Art Form

Theater improvisation

Time Required

Approximately 2 hours

Materials, Handouts, and Equipment

- One flipchart per group
- One marker per group

Procedure

1. Explain that group conversation is going to move out of our heads and "into our bodies."

2. Request a volunteer and demonstrate how you can use a person to make a statue. "Model" the volunteer with your hands. Say, "The person I am modeling is like clay, so as the 'sculptor' I can move the legs, arms, body, face, et cetera into desired positions." Do this in silence and without showing the person how to be, but by moving him or her physically. (This is based on the methods of Augusto Boal in *Theatre of the Oppressed*.)

3. Explain that larger statues can be made by modeling many people into different characters in relationship to each other. For example, two people shaking hands could be an image of greeting; two people

back-to-back could be an image of an argument. Create a small image using two people and ask the participants what they interpret it to be.

4. Ask for a volunteer to make an image that shows some of the roles people assumed during the previous activity and the relationships between those roles. This does not have to be a statue of the real situation, but should be representative of the situation.

5. When someone volunteers, ask him or her to take four or five people from the group and build the statue. The model builder must do this in silence while others in the group watch.

6. When the statue is built, invite others to alter the statue and change it into something else all can agree on (for example, people congratulating each other). Tell participants to keep conversation to a minimum in this stage and not to think or talk but to do by moving the statue.

7. After the group has completed their statue, ask: "In these types of relationships we see in the statue, what type of feelings do people have? What is inside?" Go up to one of the characters in the statue and put your hand on him or her and say what you think he or she might be feeling or thinking. Invite as many participants as would like to do this. (This deepens understanding of group dynamics.)

8. Ask: "Can we explore any of the relationships further with another small statue? For instance, can we create smaller statues about the power relationships in the team?" Ask for three or four people to volunteer to build this statue.

9. Tell the participants to create an "ideal situation" statue for a desired future state of their teams. Explain that this statue will act as a direction to walk in. It is not a destination, but more of a signpost. Ask: "What would the ideal roles and relationships be for this statue? Would anyone like to build it?" Encourage them to achieve consensus in answering these questions.

Discussion

During the final debriefing you may want to refer to the statues. These questions might help you with the discussion:

- How does this exercise help your understanding of how you work together as a group?
- What works for you already? What could you do differently?
- Based on the ideal statue, what else could this group be?

- How could you improve your group dynamics based on the outcome of this activity?
- What action plans can you as a group make and commit to? (Write these on a flipchart.)
- What implications are there for team collaboration?
- To what extent can an individual team "mold" itself into something more productive?

Contributor

Tim Merry is a partner in Engage! InterAct, an organization that encourages people to look to the benefits of difference and diversity and that helps them work together to promote and celebrate the values of respect, cooperation, and creativity. The group engages with youth, commercial, nonprofit, and governmental organizations.

TEAM MOVING

Objectives

- To better understand the strengths of a trusting and cooperative team
- To create an environment conducive to honoring the creative contribution of each team member
- To establish a climate of active participation

Uses

- Warm-up
- Team building
- Collaboration
- An icebreaker for a climate-setting workshop

Art Form

Theater improvisation

Time Required

45 to 90 minutes

Materials, Handouts, and Equipment

- A large, open room set up with chairs around the perimeter
- The following are needed for a variation of this exercise:
  - A copy of the Team Moving Questionnaire for each participant
  - Pens or pencils for each participant
  - A flipchart and markers for each group

Procedure

1. Invite the participants to walk around the room, maintaining silence. Encourage them to really explore every part of the space.
2. Explain that you will give them instructions to follow to the best of their abilities and comfort levels.

3. Have them stop moving instantly on the command, "Freeze!" They should stop in mid-motion if necessary.

4. Now introduce a number of instructions such as: "Move very quickly; very slowly; tiny steps; huge steps; move in ways as different as possible from your normal way of moving; stretch every part of your body as you move; continue this unusual way of moving in slow motion."

5. Call "Freeze" before each change. Encourage the participants to maintain balance during each freeze. Direct them to create a final, more difficult freeze to push themselves further out of balance and create a more challenging experience.

6. Finish the activity by instructing them to see if they can reach out and help each other maintain balance. Then say, "Freeze and hold!"

7. Tell them to relax and sit down on the floor or chairs.

Discussion

Lead a discussion using the following questions:

- Was it easier to take a risk when linked with another person?
- Did the workshop meet your expectations?
- What worked well? What did not work well?
- What stories of prior experiences of successful teamwork can you share with others?
- Would anyone like to share an account of projects that were difficult and unsatisfying because of ineffective teamwork?
- What have you learned about your expectations?
- What have you learned about the expectations of others?

Variations

1. Questionnaire Procedure

   - Distribute copies of the Team Moving Questionnaire and pens or pencils. Tell people not to put their names on the handout. Invite each participant to complete the questionnaire. Their responses should be quick. Don't allow too much time for well-thought-out answers.

   - Divide the participants into two groups, A and B. Collect the handouts from group A and distribute to group B; collect the handouts from group B and distribute them to group A. This redistribution should be anonymous, so shuffle each batch of handouts prior to redistributing them.

- Have each participant choose one statement from the handout that resonates for him or her. Read the chosen statements aloud one at a time to generate a "kaleidoscope" of viewpoints and attitudes regarding the group's responses to teamwork.

- Record the emerging themes and expectations on a flipchart.

2. Teamwork in Action Procedure

    - Randomly divide the participants into groups of five or six people.

    - Challenge each group to work together to create a linked, balanced configuration that is dependent on the whole group in order to be maintained. If one breaks the link, the group collapses. For instance, join hands to form a circle, then lean outward to create a linked balance. Thus if one grip slips, several people could fall. (A pyramid is not a good example because those on top can leave with no detriment to those maintaining the base.)

    - Ask each group to create two or three such formations.

    - Allow 5 to 10 minutes for this task.

    - Have each group show its best or favorite formation to the group at large.

    - If time allows or the variety is interesting, have them share all the variations.

Contributor

Born and educated in Ireland, Margaret Keane immigrated to Canada in 1967. She is a licensed associate of Mount Royal Conservatory, Calgary, and a former high school drama teacher, actor, director, and workshop facilitator. She uses her skills to inspire creativity, develop good teamwork, and enhance interpersonal skills for her clients.

Team Moving Questionnaire

Please complete the following statements:

Working as a team can often be . . .

I hesitate to contribute in a group because . . .

When in a brainstorming session, I always . . .

Many people who state they want new ideas often really want . . .

A great team needs . . .

Reproduced from *Orchestrating Collaboration at Work* by Arthur B. VanGundy & Linda Naiman with permission of the publisher. Copyright © 2005 by Arthur B. VanGundy & Linda Naiman.

TWO MINUTES OF FAME

Objectives

- To identify and compare perceptions about different company departments or divisions
- To surface "hidden" problems, obstacles, and disputes
- To determine sources of inter-departmental or inter-divisional discord
- To increase understanding of team or divisional roles, functions, and cultures

Uses

- Conflict resolution between teams or divisions
- Problem solving related to specific departments or divisions
- Communication enhancement
- Energizer

Art Form

Theater improvisation

Time Required

Approximately 1 to 2 hours, depending on number of participants and teams

Materials, Handouts, and Equipment

- Index cards, three per participant
- Pens or pencils for participants
- Copy of Two Minutes of Fame Popular Song Titles handout for each participant
- Flipchart (or white board) and markers

Procedure

1. Divide participants into small groups of four to seven people.

2. Pass out three index cards and a pen or pencil to each participant.

3. Ask each participant to briefly jot down three issues affecting different teams or divisions or conflicts between different teams or divisions (one per card). To ensure candor, tell them not to write their names on the cards. Give as examples:

   "Manufacturing doesn't understand that for the company to be competitive, timelines for Marketing's new product launches must be considerably shorter" or "Information Systems can't seem to keep up with technology changes, so our computer systems are so out-of-date."

4. Ask participants to hand in the cards. Shuffle the cards, randomly distribute three to each participant, and ask them to read all cards aloud within their subgroups.

5. Ask the participants again to hand in the cards. Let them know that you will return to these cards in a few moments, after some fun brainstorming.

6. Have them brainstorm a list of popular song titles by asking participants to shout out names of songs from any category or genre (rock, pop, soul, show tunes, sing along, holiday). Allow about 10 minutes for this activity.

7. Record all responses on a flipchart.

8. Distribute a copy of the Two Minutes of Fame Popular Song Titles handout to all participants. Allow a few minutes for participants to read the titles.

9. Explain to participants that they will be forming new subgroups and that each subgroup will be performing a 2-minute improvisation skit using themes from the song titles and team or divisional issues reviewed earlier.

10. Describe how song titles are to be used as analogies (for example, to imply similarities or differences, signify problems, suggest improvements) to jump-start and motivate the improvisation skit. Give as examples: "If Manufacturing could 'Pump Up the Volume' and complete their new product launch tasks faster, maybe Marketing could 'Break On Through' into consumers' minds and increase sales" or "Information Systems needs to be 'Blinded with Science' big time! Compared to our competitors, we are lacking in. . . ."

11. Instruct participants to divide into teams of three of four people.

12. Meanwhile, on a separate table (preferably in an uncrowded area of the room), create a "Screenwriters Idea Bank" by spreading out the issues cards face up.

13. Start with the first team and randomly assign them five song titles from the handout.

14. To select the theme of their skit, instruct the teams to choose at least one song title (from their five assigned) and to visit the "Screenwriters Idea Bank" and select one issue.

15. Tell them they must follow these rules:

    - Instead of starting the skit with one of the five assigned song titles, a wild card song title may be selected from the list of brainstormed songs.
    - Incorporating at least one song title per skit is required, but teams may include as many as they wish.
    - Paraphrasing song titles is okay, if meanings are kept (for example, "Blinded with Science" instead of "She Blinded Me with Science").
    - Humming and singing are permitted and encouraged.
    - Divisions should be the stars of the skits (such as roles, functions, cultures).
    - Imaginary props (such as an air guitar) or real props in the room (for example, door, chair, briefcase) are permitted.
    - Movement, as on a real stage, is encouraged.
    - Each improvisation must feature all team members, but everyone need not be involved in the entire 2-minute skit.

16. Remind participants that this is improvisation. As such, they will have just 2 minutes to prepare. Suggest that they use this time to determine the setting (for example, a water cooler conversation) as well as to assign acting roles to team members.

17. Direct them to freely (and naturally) add characters and other plot elements as the skit progresses in order to build an impactful and entertaining story around the divisional issue and potential solutions. (This is the essence of improvisation!)

18. Give the groups 2 minutes to prepare.

19. Ask each team to perform its skit for the entire group. Shout "Action!" to signal start. Allow each team about 2 minutes to perform.

Discussion

After all teams have performed their skits, lead a discussion summarizing the issues uncovered by using questions such as:

- How and why do you think these differences and controversies developed?

- Are problems primarily due to administrative, operational, or cultural issues?

- If you were CEO and just viewed these skits, how would you ideally like to see these divisions function, separately and together?

- To reach these ideals, what short-term and long-term changes are necessary?

- How might these divisions improve cooperation to benefit the entire company?

Contributor

Holly M. O'Neill is founder and principal of Talking Business, a marketing consultancy specializing in strategy, branding, marketing research, and product planning. By integrating creativity with structure, Talking Business delivers breakthrough concepts and solutions, which optimize clients' marketing efforts and accelerate their visionary initiatives.

Two Minutes of Fame Popular Song Titles

"A Hard Day's Night"
"Achy Breaky Heart"
"Ain't No Mountain High Enough"
"Ain't Nothing Like the Real Thing"
"Another One Bites the Dust"
"Are You Lonesome Tonight?"
"Back on the Chain Gang"
"Born to Be Wild"
"Break on Through"
"Bridge Over Troubled Water"
"Calling Occupants of Interplanetary Craft"
"Can I Get a Witness"
"Causing a Commotion"
"Day Tripper"
"Disco Inferno"
"Don't Be Cruel"
"Don't Cry for Me, Argentina"
"Don't Let the Sun Go Down on Me"
"Don't Worry, Be Happy"
"Eight Days a Week"
"Finally"
"Georgia on My Mind"
"Groove Is in the Heart"
"Help!"
"Hound Dog"
"How Sweet It Is (to Be Loved by You)"
"I Get a Kick out of You"
"I Got Rhythm"
"I Heard a Rumor"
"I Heard It Through the Grapevine"
"I Will Survive"
"I Am the Walrus"
"I'm Too Sexy"
"I've Been Working on the Railroad"
"It Came upon a Midnight Clear"
"It Don't Mean a Thing (if It Ain't Got That Swing)"
"It Takes Two"
"It's Raining Men"
"Jeepers Creepers"
"Kung Fu Fighting"
"Let's Go Crazy"
"Light My Fire"
"Like a Virgin"
"London Bridge Is Falling Down"
"Macho Man"
"Mary Had a Little Lamb"
"Me and My Shadow"
"Money (That's What I Want)"
"My Way"
"On the Sunny Side of the Street"
"Oops! I Did It Again"
"Our Lips Are Sealed"
"Pinball Wizard"
"Pump Up the Volume"
"Puppet on a String"
"Rainy Days and Mondays"
"Respect"
"Rocket Man (I Think It's Going to Be a Long, Long Time)"
"Send in the Clowns"
"(Shake, Shake, Shake) Shake Your Booty"
"She Blinded Me with Science"

Reproduced from *Orchestrating Collaboration at Work* by Arthur B. VanGundy & Linda Naiman with permission of the publisher. Copyright © 2005 by Arthur B. VanGundy & Linda Naiman.

"She'll Be Coming 'Round the Mountain"
"Start Me Up"
"Stayin' Alive"
"Stop Your Sobbing"
"Sweet Dreams (Are Made of This)"
"Tell Me Something Good"
"The Best Is Yet to Come"
"The Great Pretender"
"The Magic Touch"
"The Sound of Silence"
"The Wheels on the Bus"
"Theme from Mahogany (Do You Know Where You're Going to)"
"This Land Is Your Land"
"Three Blind Mice"
"Ticket to Ride"
"Tommy, Can You Hear Me?"
"Top of the World"
"U Can't Touch This"
"We Got the Beat"
"We Will Rock You/We Are the Champions"
"We're Not Gonna Take It"
"We've Only Just Begun"
"What a Wonderful World"
"When the Saints Go Marchin' In"
"When Will I See You Again?"
"Where Is the Love?"
"Who Let the Dogs Out?"
"Whoomp! There It Is"
"You Light Up My Life"

Reproduced from *Orchestrating Collaboration at Work* by Arthur B. VanGundy & Linda Naiman with permission of the publisher. Copyright © 2005 by Arthur B. VanGundy & Linda Naiman.

THE WORLD'S WORST LEADER

Objectives

- To identify behavior patterns associated with effective leadership
- To develop an action plan for improving personal leadership skills

Uses

- An opener in a leadership skills training session
- A closer to review leadership-skills content

Art Form

Improvisational theater

Time Required

30 to 60 minutes

Materials, Handouts, and Equipment

- A doormat or a piece of carpet placed in front of the room (to serve as the "platform")
- Flipchart and markers

Procedure

1. Before the activity, prepare a list of situations for people to act out involving dysfunctional and incompetent leaders. Examples might include scheduling an important meeting, following up on an important project, or providing feedback to a team member in front of others.

2. When the session begins, explain that you need a few volunteers for an improv theater activity. Emphasize that the activity will be a lot of fun. Ask the volunteers to stand behind the "platform," facing the audience.

3. Remind actors that they have probably worked under dysfunctional and incompetent people as their leaders. Explain that their job is to listen to a situation that you will describe, step on the platform, and act out the blundering behavior of an incompetent leader in this situation. This portrayal should be brief and comical. Actors do not have to take turns, but whoever feels ready to step on the platform should do so.

4. Begin by calling out the first situation, for example, a reporter asks for the leader's vision. Tell the actors that anyone who wants to act out the behavior of the world's worst leader in this situation should step on the platform.

5. After a reasonable time, if no actor steps on the platform, you should do it. Demonstrate a suitable (but not too brilliant) portrayal (for example, "I am not into this vision thing. I just wait for problems, immediately take charge, find the guilty person, and publicly humiliate him or her!") Then wait for the other actors to do their stuff. Applaud each portrayal.

6. After everyone has had a chance to portray the first situation, move on to the next one. (Use your prepared list or solicit suggestions from the participants.) Wait for the actors to do their portrayals.

7. Call out new and different leadership challenges. Try to cover a variety of normal and unusual situations. For a change of pace, invite audience members (and the actors) to suggest some situations.

8. Stop the drama when you feel that you have covered a sufficiently diverse set of situations. Thank the actors and lead a round of applause.

Discussion

Lead a discussion using the following questions as guides:

- What are dysfunctional behavior patterns that made the leaders appear ridiculous?
- Why were some participants reluctant to step forward?
- Is it easier to improvise within a natural work unit or team than in front of other co-workers? Why?
- What can an individual team member do if he or she believes that his or her team leader is dysfunctional?
- How easy was it to think of dysfunctional leadership patterns?

Variation

Introduce the concept of "double reversal" as a creativity technique: Have the participants flip around each dysfunctional behavior pattern to identify one or more effective leadership practices. Have participants record a list of these leadership behaviors on a flipchart. Ask each participant to identify one specific behavior pattern to implement in the near future.

Contributor

Sivasailam "Thiagi" Thiagarajan is currently the "resident mad scientist" (aka director of research and development) at QB International, an organization that specializes in designing customized learning and e-learning products. Thiagi has designed more than two hundred training games and simulations and edits a monthly online newsletter, *Play for Performance.*

12 Miscellaneous Activities

- The Blue Ribbon Panel
- Collaboration Imagination
- Here's Looking at You
- The Innovative Product Award
- Mythical Animals
- Teams in Motion

THE BLUE RIBBON PANEL

Objectives

- To help newly hired and veteran employees clarify their team cultures
- To express this understanding visually

Uses

- Values clarification
- Team building

Art Form

Design

Time Required

Approximately 15 minutes

Materials, Handouts, and Equipment

- Enough tables and chairs for each group of four to seven people (with as much space as possible between the tables)
- One set of markers, pens, and paper at each table
- Prepared overhead transparencies (see Steps 1 and 2)
- Overhead projector
- Blue award ribbons

Procedure*

1. Prepare one set of overhead transparencies in advance that use quotes such as Ralph Waldo Emerson's "A foolish consistency is the hobgoblin of little minds" or the ancient Greeks' "An unexamined life is not worth living." Any other quotes that involve assessment or evaluation also would be suitable.

---

* Note: This activity should be conducted with participants from a single organization.

2. Prepare another set of transparencies in advance that contain the following questions (one question per transparency):

   - What do you think are the core values on which this team was founded?
   - Do these values differ from the original founding values? If so, in what way?
   - What words, actions, or stories reflect the essence of your team?
   - If you had to describe the team culture in one sentence, what would you say?
   - Is there a gap in culture descriptions between management and employees? If so, how are they different?
   - Are there differences between the organizational climate and that of your work team?

3. Before the exercise, select a panel of two to three judges from within the organization to evaluate the group products.

4. Begin by using the first set of transparencies to discuss the importance of periodic team assessments.

5. Use the questions on the second set of transparencies to lead a discussion on the elements that make up the participants' current team cultures.

6. Form participants into small groups of four to seven people and ask each group to select four or five key words that represent the essence of their team.

7. Have each group design a decorative ribbon (color and design of their choice, other than blue) similar to the ribbons used to show support for hostages (yellow) or for various illnesses (red). This ribbon, however, should reflect the best elements of their existing culture. The ribbons should be drawn on a sheet of paper with the key words incorporated as desired.

8. Announce a break and invite the evaluation panel to select the symbol that best captures the principles on which the teams are based.

9. Have the panel award a blue ribbon to the team with the best ribbon design.

10. Invite the winning team members to discuss their creation and explain why they selected their color, design, words, and other creative elements.

Discussion

Lead a discussion using the following questions:

- What elements of the culture have transcended team history?
- How have technological, societal, and security issues changed the culture?
- How do your own values mesh with your team's?
- Do subcultures within the organization have their own value definitions? If so, what are they?
- If you could change the team culture in only one way, what would that be?
- What can you learn about team collaboration from this exercise? Which of these learnings are most important? Least important? Why?

Contributor

Marlene Caroselli founded the Center for Professional Development in 1984. She and her associates have conducted training throughout the United States, as well as in Singapore, Brazil, Canada, and Guam. Dr. Caroselli is the author of fifty-one books and presents training/keynotes on the topics of leadership, creativity, management, and communications.

COLLABORATION IMAGINATION

Objectives

- To exercise creativity and innovation in the design of a new product prototype
- To manage design implementation and production
- To increase awareness of the importance of participation in decision making

Uses

- Leadership
- Team building
- Communication

Art Form

Design

Time Required

- Module One: Design (1 hour)
- Module Two: Implementation (2 hours)

Materials, Handouts, and Equipment

- Tinkertoys® in a bag (one set per team plus one extra set)
- A copy of the Collaboration Imagination Instructions for each team representative and supervisor
- Ballots (enough small notepads for each participant to have one pad)
- Pens or pencils for participants
- Flipcharts and markers
- Prizes (enough candy bars or company incentives for each participant)
- A second room where some participants can meet and not be seen or heard by the remaining participants

Procedure

1. To begin Module One, explain the purpose of the exercise: To develop a design for a new product (prototype) that can be taken to market by attracting investor support. The only constraint is that they must use TinkerToys® to make the model. Their challenge is to be as creative and fanciful as possible to differentiate their product from competitors' products and to attract potential investors.

2. Organize the participants into teams of five and provide each team with a set of TinkerToys®.

3. Tell the teams that they have 20 minutes to work out the design for this product and make a business case to investors to raise capital. Each team should prepare a 2-minute "pitch" by identifying its target market, why they would want this product, and why it is a good investment. Remind them to be imaginative and fanciful. During this time, each team also will produce its prototype.

4. Ask each team to present its "pitch" to the whole group. Ensure that the time constraints are maintained (perhaps by commencing applause once 2 minutes have expired).

5. Distribute notepads and pens or pencils to all participants and ask each participant to vote for the best product and pitch by writing the name of the product on a sheet of paper. Participants may not vote for their own products.

6. Collect and tally the votes while conducting the debriefing. (See questions in the Discussion section.)

7. Summarize the discussion, congratulate the top vote-getting team, and present them an award. Tell participants that there will be a 5-minute break. During this break, carry all of the prototypes and the extra set of unused TinkerToys® into the second room.

8. After the break, begin Module Two. Explain to the participants that you now will act in the role of investor and, as investor, you liked the potential of many of the prototypes and would like to meet with a representative from each group to discuss their proposals.

9. Ask each group to nominate a representative to meet with you.

10. Prepare to take the team representatives to the second room. Ensure that the other participants cannot see or hear the discussion. Prior to leaving the main room, instruct the remaining participants to nominate a supervisor for each group. The supervisors will meet with their group representative once they have finished with you. (*Note to trainer:* There is a period of 5 to 10 minutes during which the remaining participants are kept in the dark. It is an intentional tension builder. Be vague and brief and advise people that their "supervisor" will soon be providing more information.)

11. Once in the second room with the team reps, explain that you will invest only if certain design elements can be incorporated. Select design features from each of the prototypes to come up with a hybrid product. Distribute the TinkerToys® and have the representatives create this hybrid together using the extra set of TinkerToys®, giving them 5 minutes.

12. Place the hybrid prototype in a location that conceals it from the sight of the supervisors who will be visiting the representatives. To conceal the module, consider simple, movable partitions, flipcharts, or a hallway. Ask the team reps to disassemble the prototypes (not the hybrid) and return each set of TinkerToys® to its bag.

13. Return to the main room, gather the "supervisors," and tell them to join you and the team reps in the second room. Once in the second room, explain what has preceded their arrival. (*Note:* The hybrid prototype should be out of sight from the supervisors at all times.)

14. Tell the team reps that, because they shared in creating the prototype, you (the investor) are going to give them all the opportunity to win the contract for the mass production of this new product. The contract will be awarded to the team that produces an *exact replica* of the prototype in the *shortest amount of time*. The team that can do this will have demonstrated that they are the best in terms of timeliness and quality—both critical attributes for the supplier to show.

15. Ask each supervisor to pick up a bag of TinkerToys®. Return to the main room with the reps and supervisors.

16. Distribute the Collaboration Imagination Instructions to the supervisors and group representatives and start the competition.

17. After 5 minutes, ask workers, "Have you ever had a similar experience in the workplace? For those who have, please describe that experience to your group."

18. Encourage them to continue this table group discussion until their supervisors tell them to start building. (*Note:* Sit in on several of the discussions. The goal of this debriefing intervention is to create optimal engagement of the workers in what could be a very boring 20 minutes. Five minutes usually is enough for workers to experience the brain-numbing state the activity is designed to create.)

19. Involve the participants in judging which group has been most successful using the criteria of quality (zero defects) and timeliness (the quickest time).

20. Conclude by stating, "We missed the goal in this last activity." Acknowledge that the supervisors and representatives were "set up," since the activity was structured almost to guarantee a compromised experience. Thank the supervisors and representatives.

Discussion (Module One)

These questions should be addressed before the break:

- How did you feel as a result of collaboration?
- What happened?
- How effectively did you collaborate?
- Did everyone have a voice and was everyone heard?
- What were the enablers of creativity?
- What were the barriers to creativity?
- Do you see any parallels with respect to workplace dynamics?
- Even though the inventions are fanciful, what are some practical applications?

Discussion (Module Two)

Facilitate a post-exercise discussion using the following questions. (Facilitator instructions are in brackets.)

- What is one word to describe the predominant feeling from the planning phase of the activity? [Record six to eight words on flipchart.]
- Who has seen parallels in the real world? [Ask for a show of hands.]
- What is the impact or cost of this type of workplace?
- What was the impact of inclusion or omission of your input in the hybrid? [Allow at least 2 minutes for a small group discussion and 30 seconds for group reports.]
- What is one word that you would like to have your people choose to describe your workplace? [Record six to eight words on a flipchart corresponding to the previous list.]
- What is a leader's role in implementation? [Optional: Conduct a small group discussion for 5 minutes. Allow 1 minute for small group reports.]
- What is the most important message you are taking away from the session? [Allow several participants to respond as time permits.]

Close by noting that a leader's role is to (1) distinguish between getting results and how you get results and (2) create an optimal process that enables a unique group of people to do its best work.

Contributors

Alex Wray, principal of Facilitation Training Inc., is a consultant and facilitator to senior and middle management in the areas of strategy and strategic issues and challenges. Clients include the CEO's offices of Motorola Inc. and Ford Motor Company. A practical, insightful, and trustworthy advisor, Wray is a powerful catalyst for individual and organizational change.

Linda Naiman, BFA, works with organizations to awaken genius-level thinking through the art and science of applying creativity, innovation, and visionary thinking to business strategy. Naiman is a life-long artist and presents workshops on creativity and innovation in North America and Europe.

Collaboration Imagination Instructions

Goal: Assemble an exact duplicate of the Hybrid Prototype that the investor has approved in the shortest amount of time.

Planning (20 minutes)

1. The table group representative is the only person who can go and see the model.
2. The table group representative can go and see the model as many times as needed.
3. The table group representative communicates how to construct the prototype to the supervisor.
4. The supervisor is the only one who can write and draw.
5. At any time during the planning, the supervisor can brief and prepare his or her workers for the assembly.
6. During the planning phase, no one can touch the Tinkertoy® pieces. If the pieces are taken out of the bag, the team will be in violation of ISO 9002 quality standards; if a competitor reports this to the investor, the entire team will be disqualified from the competition.
7. Under no circumstances is pre-assembly permitted.

Assembly (Maximum of 7 minutes)

1. Prior to commencing, all pieces must be in the bag.
2. When assembly begins, the table group representative cannot go back to see the model.
3. When assembly begins, only the workers can touch the pieces.
4. The supervisor can instruct the workers, but cannot touch the pieces.
5. The table group representative can watch the assembly. If he or she wants to give a supervisor more information (for example, to correct an error), the table group representative must call the supervisor off the job. The table group representative cannot talk with the workers or be overheard by the workers.

Reproduced from *Orchestrating Collaboration at Work* by Arthur B. VanGundy & Linda Naiman with permission of the publisher. Copyright © 2005 by Arthur B. VanGundy & Linda Naiman.

HERE'S LOOKING AT YOU

Objectives

- To understand how perceptions vary within teams
- To determine specific perceptions of individual group members
- To demonstrate how individual and group perceptions differ

Uses

- Team building
- Visioning
- Leadership
- Nonverbal communication

Art Form

Photography

Time Required

- Five work days to collect photos
- Approximately 1 hour for discussion

Materials, Handouts, and Equipment

- Pre-session
  - Camcorder or digital camera
  - Printer for photos (or commercial developer)
  - Computer (optional)
- During session
  - Flipchart (or a computer) for each group
  - Markers for each group
  - Computer projector (optional)

Procedure

1. Before the scheduled session, select intact work teams to participate. For large teams, break them into subgroups of five people each. Other teams in an organization also could participate if time and other resources are available.

2. Explain to participants that this activity is designed to demonstrate differences in perceptions and how different perspectives and elements (for example, light, framing, contrast) can affect those differences.

3. Provide each team member with a camcorder or digital camera. If necessary, provide training on how to use the cameras. Individual members can use their own personal cameras or share with others. If cameras are shared, create a schedule so that each person will have access to one camera for at least 30 minutes every day for at least five working days.

4. Tell each participant to take a minimum of ten pictures involving other team members in different situations (for example, at their desks, in meetings, at lunch, during informal conversations, on breaks). These pictures should reflect a variety of settings. Obtain any permission required to take random photos of individuals or a work team. Also obtain permission from all participants to have their pictures taken.

5. Establish a designated time by which all pictures must be completed and developed or uploaded to computers for projection on the day of the session.

6. After all of the pictures have been developed or loaded onto computers for projection, assemble the teams together and have each team's members share their pictures individually with other team members. Have them first focus on describing what they see, what is going on, any implied emotions, work-related versus personal-related behaviors, et cetera. Encourage them to solicit feedback from others and discuss similarities and differences between the pictures of different team members.

7. Have a recorder write down their observations on a flipchart.

8. Tell the teams to continue sharing pictures and recording comments until all pictures have been described and discussed. Ask the recorders to summarize the results in writing.

9. If more than one team is involved, convene all groups to share their reactions by having one person from each group share the summarized results.

Discussion

Use the following questions to facilitate a discussion involving all participating teams:

- How similar or different were the individual pictures of the same settings and people?
- Were the differences pronounced? Why or why not?
- What implications can you draw from the individual differences?
- Some research indicates that we communicate with others more when using nonverbal messages than verbal ones. What examples of nonverbal communication did you observe (hand gestures, facial expressions, body posture)?
- What effect, if any, do these nonverbal communications have on team collaboration?
- What differences exist between teams in either the general photographic images or in their nonverbal communications? Are these expected differences? Why did you expect them? Why not?
- Based on this discussion, what conclusions can you make about team collaboration?

Variation

Collect images one or two days a month over a six-month period and then analyze the pictures for changes over time. Discuss why the changes occurred.

Contributor

Arthur VanGundy, Ph.D., works as a creativity consultant, trainer, and facilitator of brainstorming retreats. He is the author of ten books, including *Techniques of Structured Problem Solving, Training Your Creative Mind, Managing Group Creativity, Brain Boosters for Business Advantage,* and *101 Great Games & Activities.* Major clients include Hershey Foods, S.C. Johnson Company, Xerox, Motorola, Sunbeam, Air Canada, Monsanto, Wyeth-Ayerst Pharmaceuticals, and the Singapore government. He also is founder of All Star Minds, a global Internet brainstorming service.

THE INNOVATIVE PRODUCT AWARD

Objectives

- To provide a fun, hands-on experience of new product invention
- To help participants create spontaneously using limited resources

Uses

- Creativity
- Problem solving
- Selling ideas
- Team building
- A culminating training exercise

Art Form

Design

Time Required

Approximately 2 hours

Materials, Handouts, and Equipment

- Cardboard boxes
- Empty egg and milk cartons
- Plastic bottles
- Several rolls of tape (duct, masking, and cellophane)
- Staplers
- Wire and wire cutters
- Needles and thread
- Goop® and epoxy glue
- Balls of yarn
- String
- Rolls of colored tissue paper, ribbons
- One box of cloth remnants

- Sewing and stationery odds and ends
- An assortment of colorful stickers—enough for all participants to share
- Colored markers and glitter pens
- A table on which to display the inventions
- An index card for each team
- A ballot for each participant (see Step 9)
- A pen or pencil for each participant
- Prizes for the winning team (simple novelty items)

Procedure

1. Divide the participants into small groups of four to seven people.
2. Arrange chairs into a circle for each small group.
3. Place the materials on the floor in the center of a circle of chairs where the participants will take their places.
4. Explain that the purpose of the activity is to experience creativity within a prescribed time limit and in a competitive environment.
5. Tell participants that they have 1 hour to use the materials to create a product that will receive their company's "Innovative Product of the Year" award.
6. Tell them to begin.
7. Call time and advise them that their invention has been entered into a national competition with a big, secret prize. Tell each group to name its product, describe and demonstrate its uses to the large group, explain why it won the company competition, and explain why it deserves to win the national competition.
8. After the presentations, ask each group to write the name of its invention on an index card and place the card with the product on an "exhibition" table.
9. Hand out individual ballots with the numbers "1," "2," and "3" listed. Instruct participants to review the inventions displayed and vote for the top three, in order of preference (1 = most preferred and 3 = least preferred). (Individuals may not vote for their own inventions.) Have a volunteer from the group collect the ballots, tally the results, and report the winner.
10. Present awards to the winning team.

Discussion

Facilitate a discussion using the following questions as guides:

- When did you actually get the idea for your product?
- Was it prompted internally or by other participants?
- Did your creation change from your original idea? If so, in what way?
- How difficult was it to transform your idea into a three-dimensional form?
- Did you have any anxious moments during the process? If so, what were they and when did they occur?
- Did the time limit and competition inspire or inhibit you?
- What was most interesting to you about this activity?
- What did you like most? Least?
- How can you apply this to creative problem solving and innovation in your workplace?
- What implications are there for team collaboration?

Contributor

Jacqueline Gautier, B.A.C., is an international creativity consultant, keynote speaker, and author. She specializes in facilitating workshops on Thinking Ahead of the Box and presents a series of courses on Creativity and Wellness. Her recent book, *Treasure: Creative Adventures in Self-Discovery*, reached bestseller status in Saskatchewan, Canada, in November 2001.

MYTHICAL ANIMALS

Objectives

- To create a mascot for your team, department, or company
- To demonstrate the value of multiple perspectives
- To create a metaphor for change/team/mission
- To think with your hands

Uses

- Creative thinking
- Group identity
- Community building
- Corporate culture
- Collaboration

Art Form

Sculpture

Time Required

60 minutes

Materials, Handouts, and Equipment

- One can or box of modeling clay or Play-Doh® for each participant

Procedure

1. Divide the participants into subgroups of four to seven people.

2. Read this quote from sculptor Henry Moore: "Sculpture is like a journey. You have a different view as you return. The three-dimensional world is full of surprises in a way that a two-dimensional world could never be."

3. Note that mythical creatures were traditionally symbols of the polarity of human nature or our union with nature. Examples of mythical animals include the Minotaur, sphinx, unicorn, centaurs, sirens, and mermaids. Note that numerous companies and many sports teams use animals as mascots: "Charlie Tuna" and the Miami Dolphins are two examples. Ask the groups to think of other examples.

4. Ask each subgroup to create a clay sculpture by inventing a mythical animal of its own and to think of it as a metaphor for their team (or organization). Instruct them to think three-dimensionally so that, like Henry Moore's, the sculpture is interesting visually no matter what the angle. The sculpture should be at least 4 inches in height.

5. Have everyone display their mythical animals and tell a story about what they represent. Let the entire group decide whether it wants to vote on its favorite and have an official mascot.

Discussion

Lead a discussion using the following questions:

- What do these animals say about you as individuals and as teams?
- What themes emerged in the storytelling and in the choice of animals?
- What characteristics of the animals seemed to be most important?
- What do these characteristics have to do with team collaboration?
- How might your team use its mascot to improve team performance, morale, or some other team-related issue?

Variation

Rather than using subgroups, each individual could create his or her own sculpture.

Contributor

Linda Naiman, BFA, works with organizations to awaken genius-level thinking through the art and science of applying creativity, innovation, and visionary thinking to business strategy. Naiman is a life-long artist and presents workshops on creativity and innovation in North America and Europe.

TEAMS IN MOTION

Objectives

- To foster group awareness and collaboration
- To energize participants through movement to music

Uses

- Warm-up
- Icebreaker
- Team building

Art Form

Dance

Time Required

10 to 15 minutes

Materials, Handouts, and Equipment

- A tape or CD player
- A lively piece of music on tape or CD (check copyright restrictions)

Procedure

1. Form groups of five to eight people, standing in a spacious area.

2. Ask each participant to connect to his or her group physically by touching two other people in the group. They may hold hands, touch someone's arm, back, or any two points of contact that would be appropriate. Demonstrate possible ways of touching while explaining what they should do. (In cultures where touching is improper, participants can hold either end of small scarves to connect.)

3. Have one person in each group disconnect from the rest of the group, stand nearby, but remain physically detached from the others.

4. Explain that when the music begins, each group should move across the floor, with the members remaining in two-point contact. Only one member may be disconnected from the group at a time. The one who starts off disconnected then should reconnect while another member simultaneously disconnects. Only one person may be out at one time, and it may not be the same person throughout.

5. Start the music and encourage the groups to begin moving around the room. Coach the individuals and groups to reconnect and disconnect as necessary.

6. End the exercise by turning off the music.

Discussion

Lead a discussion using the following questions:

- Did you prefer to stick with your group or detach?
- Did your group have more members who wanted to stick together or more who wanted to detach?
- How did it feel when you were separate from your group? When you rejoined them?
- Did your group successfully meet the objective of having one and only one person out at all times?
- If so, what happened to allow that? If not, what happened to prevent that?
- What else did you notice?
- What did you learn from this experience?
- How might you apply what you learned to team collaboration?

Variations

1. Play different kinds of music—from slow and meditative to quick and lively—to see how type of music influences a group's ability to remain in synch. This variation will take more time than the basic exercise.

2. You can vary both the size of the groups and the number of people who are disconnected from each group at any one time.

3. For icebreaking purposes, have the disconnected person reconnect, but not with his or her original group. Instead have them reconnect with a different group so that group composition continues to change throughout the exercise.

Contributor

Jacquie Lowell, M.Ed., has been leading creativity and improvisational comedy workshops for twenty-five years. Drawing on experience in theater, dance, psychology, and metaphysics, she has developed lively creativity-stimulating exercises and training programs for companies, organizations, conferences, and schools. She also directs the Creative Urges and Mission Improvible improvisational comedy troupes.

13 Evaluation Activities

- Artistic Insights
- Song Lyrics
- Symbolic Solutions

ARTISTIC INSIGHTS

Objectives

- To identify key insights from a training workshop or activity
- To develop action plans from training insights

Uses

- A closing activity after a training workshop
- A debriefing activity after a specific training activity or game

Art Form

Drawing

Time Required

40 to 60 minutes

Materials, Handouts, and Equipment

- A large sheet of drawing paper for each participant
- Large boxes of crayons of different colors—one box per table
- Timer

Procedure

1. Divide participants into equal-sized teams of four to six members each. Seat team members around a table.

2. Ask participants to think back silently on what happened during the training workshop or activity. Invite them to close their eyes and visualize the highlights of the event. After a suitable pause, ask participants to think silently of one or more insights they received from the event.

3. Place sheets of drawing paper and boxes of crayons in the middle of each table. Ask each participant to take a sheet of paper and to share the crayons.

4. Ask each participant to draw an abstract picture that captures the essence of major insights from the training event. Encourage them not to worry about artistic quality, but to flow with their intuitive thoughts and feelings. Announce a 10-minute time limit for this task and set the timer.

5. At the end of 10 minutes, ask the participants to stop drawing. Reassure them that it does not matter if the drawing is not yet complete.

6. At each table, ask participants to take turns holding up the picture. While doing this, ask each person who is holding up the picture to remain quiet (a difficult task!). Invite other participants around the table to treat the picture as a Rorschach inkblot and interpret what insights they see in it. Participants don't have to take turns presenting their insights. Anyone may call out interpretations whenever he or she feels inspired.

7. After all the pictures have been interpreted, ask the table teams to repeat the process. This time, however, each person should hold up his or her picture and describe what insights he or she meant to convey.

Discussion

After the sharing of insights, encourage a discussion at each table. Use such questions as:

- Were there differences in interpretations between others' descriptions and your own interpretation? What were they and why do you think they occurred?
- What insights were mentioned most frequently?
- What insights were unexpected and unique?
- What was the most powerful insight that affected you?
- How do you expect this insight to change your future behavior?
- How might your team use its insights to improve team collaboration and performance?

Contributor

Sivasailam "Thiagi" Thiagarajan is currently the "resident mad scientist" (aka director of research and development) at QB International, an organization that specializes in designing customized learning and e-learning products. Thiagi has designed more than two hundred training games and simulations and edits a monthly online newsletter, *Play for Performance*.

SONG LYRICS

Objectives

- To engage team participants holistically
- To provide metaphors for a training topic
- To create a multi-dimensional overview of a training topic

Uses

- A starting point for any discussion topic
- Fostering and enhancing discussion about a training topic
- Evaluating training outcomes

Art Form

Music

Time Required

15 minutes

Materials, Handouts, and Equipment

- CD player
- CDs with the selected songs (check copyright restrictions)
- Song lyric sheets (check copyright restrictions)

Procedure

1. Select pop songs that relate to the training topic. For example, "Respect," "You're So Vain," "Lyin' Eyes" and "Macarena" all could be used for a discussion about sexual harassment.

2. Divide the participants into small groups of four to seven people and assign a song to each group. Distribute the appropriate lyric sheets to each group.

3. Ask the groups to determine how the song relates to the training topic. Allow 5 minutes for group discussion.

4. Bring the participants back together. Ask each group, in turn, to share ways in which their songs relate to the training topic. When there is a break in the discussion, play the song (or a portion if time is limited).

5. Thank all the groups for their observations.

6. Remind the participants of the discussion and play the songs again at incidental moments during the training.

Discussion

Lead a discussion using the following questions:

- How did your song relate to the training topic?
- Were you surprised at the relationship?
- How do all these songs relate to the topic?
- How are those relationships similar? Different?
- How do those relationships add to your knowledge of the subject?
- What conclusions can you draw from this information?

Variations

1. Assign the activity as homework.
2. Ask the participants to find a song relating to the topic and bring it to the next session.

Contributor

Lenn Millbower is the author of *Training with a Beat, Cartoons for Trainers, Show Biz Training,* and *Game Show Themes for Trainers.* He is a magician, a music arranger, a pianist, an instructional designer, and an educator who combines entertainment and learning into interventions that are creative, meaningful, and fun.

SYMBOLIC SOLUTIONS

Objectives

- To capture unconscious symbolic information
- To weave that information into stories containing problem insights or solutions

Uses

- Training evaluation
- Communication
- Team building
- Problem solving

Art Form

Storytelling

Time Required

Approximately 60 minutes

Materials, Handouts, and Equipment

- Enough butcher paper to cover all tables used
- Enough masking tape to tape the paper to the tables
- One box of crayons or colored pencils for each participant
- One flipchart
- One flipchart marker

Procedure*

1. Set up the room in advance of the session by taping the paper to the tables, completely covering the surface. Distribute the crayons or colored pencils so that everyone has a box.

---

* Note: This activity may work best as an evaluation at the end of a training day with small groups of four to six people working around small tables.

2. Encourage everyone to doodle throughout the training day (or a specific session), just as one would do when talking on the telephone. Even if people do not normally doodle, tell them it will help stimulate their creative juices and involve their right brains in the activities of the day. Make it fun and lighthearted. Check on the participants' doodles and make encouraging comments to keep them going throughout the session.

3. Toward the end of the day or session—about 90 minutes before wrap-up—divide people into small groups of four to six people if they are not already in groups.

4. Tell the overall group that the buried treasure of their unconscious minds is present but hidden within the doodles on the tables. Their job is to come up with a story based on the doodles that relates to the subject of the session.

5. Have everyone circulate throughout the room for approximately 5 minutes to look at all the doodles.

6. Once they have viewed the doodles, ask them to convene in small groups and give them 10 minutes to come up with a story based on the doodles. Instruct them to use their full imaginations to incorporate their interpretation of the doodles into any form of story they choose. However, the story must have a moral.

7. Give one person from each group 3 minutes to share their story and its moral with the overall group. (Ask people to take a "quantum leap" to look for how the stories and morals relate to the overall subject/issue of the session.)

8. Write the morals on the flipchart as the stories are told.

9. Distill the central messages or insights for the group to take away and discuss how these ideas and insights might be developed further and any practical applications.

Discussion

The following questions can be used to help guide the discussion:

- What effect did this exercise have on the energy level of the participants?

- To what extent did the doodles help synthesize or summarize the session's content?

- Were some doodles more descriptive than others? In what way? Why would this be?

- Did any of the doodles symbolically represent profound insights? Hidden content or feelings?
- Were there any covert or overt messages conveyed by the doodles? If so, what were they and what do they mean?
- What role do "hidden agendas" play in creating the doodles?
- What implications, if any, are there for using doodles to enhance team collaboration?

Variations

1. Offer a prize for the most prolific doodler—not for the best artwork.
2. Offer a prize for the most inventive moral to the story.

Contributor

Gael McCool, Ph.D., is a behavioral consultant and teacher in the Vancouver, B.C., area. In her practice, Dr. McCool has consulted with and provided training to such companies as the Walt Disney Company, Johnson & Johnson, and several television networks. She is currently on sabbatical writing a book, *Emotional Accountability*.

Contributor Contact Information

James Barnes
JB Innovation
112 Banbury Way
Wayne, PA 19087
Phone: 215–435–2705
Email: James@jbinnovation.com
URL: www.jbinnovation.com

Dick Baumbusch
President
The Knowledge Advantage Group
Phone: 303–663–5464
Fax: 303–663–0021
Email: rbaumbusch@mba1974.hbs.edu

Lena Bjørn
The Dacapo Theatre
Kongensgade 66–68
5000 Odense
Denmark
Phone: 0045–66147146
Fax: 0045–66147145
Email: lb@dacapoteatret.dk
URL: www.dacapoteatret.dk

Gervase Bushe
Faculty of Business
Simon Fraser University
Burnaby, BC V5A 1B6
Canada
Phone: 604–291–4104
Email: bushe@sfu.ca
URL: www.gervasebushe.com

Marlene Caroselli
Center for Professional Development
324 Latona Road, Suite 1600
Rochester, NY 14626
Phone: 716-227–6512
Fax: 509–696–5405
Email: mccpd@aol.com

John J. Cimino, Jr.
President & CEO
Creative Leaps International
731 Sprout Brook Road
Putnam Valley, NY 10579
Phone: 845–528–5908
Email: jcimino@westnet.com
URL: www.creativeleaps.org

Nan Crawford, M.A.
President and Artistic Director
Nan Crawford & Co., Pacific Playback Theatre
4104 24th Street, #777
San Francisco, CA 94114
Phone: 415–282–8558
Fax: "Attn: Nan Crawford"
  415–824–1072
Email: nan@nancrawford.com
URL: www.nancrawford.com

Lisa DeVuono
Artist Conference Network
637 North Bishop Avenue
Springfield, PA 19064
Phone: 610–328–1029
Email: LDeVuono@hotmail.com

John Fox
P.O. Box 60189
Palo Alto, CA 94306
Phone: 650–938–2717
Email: jfoxcpt@aol.com
URL: www.poeticmedicine.com

Jacqueline Gautier, B.A.C.
Jacqueline Gautier & Associates
1701 Arlington Avenue
Saskatoon, SK S7H 2Y6
Canada
Phone: 306–374–6592
Fax: 306–477–3489
Email: jgautier@sk.sympatico.ca
URL: www.jgautier.com

Conni Gordon, CPS, CEO
Gordon Global Creative Institute
427 22nd Street
Miami Beach, FL 33139-1706
Phone: 305–532–1001
Email: connigordn@aol.com

Bonnie Goren
Phone: 425–706–9923
Email: bonniegoren2002@msn.com

Deborah Jacroux
Phone: 831–624–4253
Email: deborahbaraka@earthlink.net

Seth Weaver Kahan
President
Performance Development Group, Inc.
P.O. Box 380
Glen Echo, MD 20812
Phone: 301–229–2221
Fax: 301–229–6661
Email: Seth@SethKahan.com
URL: www.sethkahan.com

Jerry Kail
Senior Organization Development Consultant
LexisNexis
9443 Springboro Pike
Dayton, OH 47342
Phone: 937–865–1823
Fax: 937–847–3090
Email: jerry.kail@lexisnexis.com

Margaret Keane
Drama and Speech Coach
Power Surge Theatre
3151 East 21st Avenue
Vancouver, BC V5M 2W8
Canada
Phone: 604–433–8008
Email: margaret_keane@yahoo.co.uk

Janice Kilgore
Southwest Music Enterprises, LLC
317 Oak Meadow Lane
Cedar Hill, TX 75104
Phone: 972–291–9130
Fax: 972–291–4361
Email: jkkmusik@aol.com

Michele and Frank Lewski
Phone: 732–946–4736
Email: mlewski@juno.com

Jacquie Lowell
Founder and CFO (Creative Fun Officer)
Creativity Games
3766 Southview Drive, Suite 250
San Diego, CA 92117-5338
Phone: 858–581–0050
Email: jlowell.improv@juno.com
URL: www.jacquielowell.com

Gael McCool, Ph.D.
Behavioral Consultant
12666 14 B Avenue
Surrey, BC V4A 1J6
Canada
Phone: 604–542–2490
Email: gaelmccool@shaw.ca

Tim Merry
Partner
Engage! Interact
Bemuude Weerd WZ 3
Utrecht 3513BH
Netherlands
Phone: +31 (0) 30 251 3182
Fax: + 31 (0) 30 238 7517
Email: tim@engage.nu

Lenn Millbower
President
Offbeat Training®
329 Oakpoint Circle
Davenport, FL 33837
Phone: 407–256–0501
Email: lennmillbower@offbeattraining.com

Gary Muszynski
One World Music
5245 College Ave., #326
Oakland, CA 94618
Phone: 800-930-8812
Fax: 888-863-2007
Email: gary@oneworldmusic.com

Linda Naiman
Linda Naiman & Associates Inc.
2181 West 38th Avenue, Suite 804
Vancouver, BC V6M 1R8
Canada
Phone: 604–327–1565
Email: info@creativityatwork.com
URL: www.creativityatwork.com

Jan Nickerson
The Prosperity Collaborative, Inc.
222 Old Connecticut Path
Wayland, MA 01778
Phone: 508–358–7146
Fax: 508–358–7247
Email: jannickerson@attbi.com

Nick Nissley
University of St. Thomas
Mail # MOH 217
1000 La Salle Avenue
Minneapolis, MN 55403–2009
Phone: 651–962–4983
Email: nnissley@stthomas.edu

Richard Olivier
Olivier Mythodrama Associates Ltd.
273 Fulham Palace Road
Fulham, London SW6 6TL
England, UK
Phone: 0044 20 7386 7972
Fax: 0044 20 7386 9763
Email: info@oliviermythodrama.com
URL: www.oliviermythodrama.com

Holly M. O'Neill
Principal
Talking Business
P.O. 14218
Irvine, CA 92623
Phone: 949–477–4020
Fax: 949–477–4021
Email: holly.oneill@att.net

David Pearl
Experience Engineering™
Email: connect@davidpearl.co.uk

Miha Pogacnik
Phone/Fax: (++49) 40 485158
Email: mihaidriart@attglobal.net
URL: www.speakers.co.uk
www.washingtonspeakers.com
www.mihapogacnik.com
www.idriart.org

Carla Rieger
Director
YES Education Systems
#138 – 2906 West Broadway
Vancouver, BC V6K 2G3
Canada
Phone: 604–267–2381
Fax: 604–222–2276
Email: info@yeseducationsystems.com

Bob Root-Bernstein, Ph. D.
Professor of Physiology
Michigan State University
East Lansing, MI 48824
Phone: 517–355–6475 ext 1101
Email: rootbern@msu.edu

John Seely Brown
Email: jsb@parc.com

Todd Siler, Ph.D.
Think Like a Genius, LLC
6555 S. Kenton Street, Suite 304
Englewood, CO 80111
Phone: 303–649–9388
Fax: 303–649–9236
Email: tsiler@thinklikeagenius.com
URL: www.thinklikeagenius.com

Sivasailam Thiagarajan, Ph.D.
QB International
4423 East Trailridge Road
Bloomington, IN 47408
Phone: 812–332–1478
Email: thiagi@thiagi.com
URL: www.thiagi.com

Paul Smith
Regional Director
Arts & Business North West
Portland Buildings, 1C
127–129 Portland Street
Manchester M1 4PZ
England, UK
Email: paul.smith@aandb.org.uk
URL: www.AandB.org.uk

Arthur VanGundy, Ph.D.
428 Laws Drive
Norman, OK 73072–3851
Phone: 405–447–1946
Email: avangundy@cox.net
URL: www.allstarminds.com

Margaret Wheatley
The Berkana Institute
P.O. Box 1407
Provo, Utah 84603
Phone: 801-377-2996
Email: info@berkana.org

David Whyte
Many Rivers Press
P.O. Box 868
Langley, WA 98260
Phone: 360–221–1324
Email: mrivers@davidwhyte.com
URL: www.davidwhyte.com

Lola Wilcox
Leadership and Change Management
StorageTek
1 StorageTek Drive—MS 3256
Louisville, CO 80028–3256
Phone: 303–661–5447
Email: wilcoll@louisville.stortek.com

Alex Wray
President
Facilitation Training Inc. (FTI)
5363 Westhaven Wynd
West Vancouver, BC V7W 3E8
Canada
Phone: 604–921–1316
Fax: 604–921–1341
Email: alex@facilitationtraining.com
URL: www.facilitationtraining.com

About the Editors

Arthur B. (Andy) VanGundy Ph.D.

Arthur VanGundy is Professor of Communication at the University of Oklahoma and President of VanGundy & Associates, specializing in idea generation. He has over 35 years experience in higher education and idea generation training and facilitation. He is considered a pioneer in his work on idea generation techniques and has written 15 books including: *Techniques of Structured Problem Solving* (1981), *108 Ways to Get a Bright Idea* (1983), *101 Creativity and Problem Solving Activities* (2005), and *Getting to Innovation: How Asking the Right Questions Generates the Great Ideas Your Company Needs*.

His clients include: Air Canada, Hershey Foods, MBNA, Monsanto, S.C. Johnson & Sons, the Singapore government, and Sunbeam. Dr. VanGundy has received leadership service awards from the Creative Education Foundation and the Singapore government, is "Chief Framer" for the Global Innovation Challenge, and serves on the board of directors of Creative Oklahoma, Inc.

Contact information:

Arthur VanGundy
428 Laws Drive, Norman,
OK 73072.
Tel: +1 (405) 447- 1946,
email: avangundy@cox.net.

Linda Naiman

Linda Naiman is recognized internationally for pioneering arts-based learning and its application in developing creativity, collaboration, teamwork and leadership in organizations. Her work has been documented on *TU Danmark* TV and in several books: *Artbased Approaches: A Practical Handbook to Creativity at Work* (Chemi 2006), *Wake Me Up When the Data Is Over: How Organizations Use Stories to Drive Results* (Silverman 2006), and *Artful Creation: Learning Tales of Arts-in-Business* (Darsø 2004). She has also been featured in *The Vancouver Sun, The Globe and Mail, Canadian Business Magazine, CMO Magazine, Profitguide.com, CBC Radio,* and *National Public Radio.*

Linda is an associate business coach at the University of British Columbia, and an adjunct faculty member of the Banff Centre Leadership Lab. She conducts workshops and facilitates arts-based dialogue in North America, Europe and Asia. Clients include AstraZeneca, BP International, Benjamin Moore, Fairmont Hotels, and Radical Entertainment.

Linda holds a BFA from California College of the Arts, a diploma in Graphic Design from Emily Carr Institute of Art + Design, and business coaching certification from Corporate Coach University. She is a life-long artist whose mission is to make life and work a work of art.

For details about workshops, retreats, meeting facilitation, and coaching visit www.creativityatwork.com.

Contact information:

Linda Naiman
Corporate Alchemist

Turning leaden thinking into gold through
Consulting, Coaching and Training.

Linda Naiman & Associates Inc
2181 West 38th Ave, Suite 804
Vancouver BC Canada V6M 1R8
Tel: +1 (604) 327-1565

www.creativityatwork.com
email: LN@creativityatwork.com

Subscribe to the Creativity at Work Newsletter online.

CPSIA information can be obtained at www.ICGtesting.com
Printed in the USA
270230BV00006B/35/P